Is He Coming Soon?

A Reader's Guide To The Book Of Revelation

Dean J. Piper

CSS Publishing Company, Inc., Lima, Ohio

IS HE COMING SOON?

Library of Congress Cataloging-in-Publication Data

Piper, Dean J., 1939-
Is He coming soon? : a reader's guide to the Book of Revelation / Dean J. Piper.
p. cm.
ISBN 0-7880-1336-X (pbk.)
1. Bible. N.T. Revelation—Commentaries. I. Title.
BS2825.3.P57 1999
228'.07—dc21 98-44911
CIP

ISBN 0-7880-1336-X PRINTED IN U.S.A.

*To the Adult Bible Classes who
encouraged me over the past thirty years
to teach from this book, and to my pastor friends
who requested a simple and usable study of this
mystifying Revelation of Jesus Christ to Saint John.*

Table Of Contents

Preface

You are about to begin reading one of the least read and most misunderstood books of the Bible. This Reader's Guide is designed to be read side by side with the Book of Revelation. After you have finished reading the introductory chapter of this book on Apocalyptic Literature and understanding the Book of Revelation, you must do one more thing before jumping into the Book of Revelation. You must read either Mark 13, Matthew 24:1-51, or Luke 21:5-36. These are Gospel accounts of Jesus' earthly teachings about the end of time and final judgment. If we don't read the Book of Revelation in the light of Jesus' earthly teachings, then we make The Book of Revelation an end unto itself and subject it to the possibility of total misinterpretation. Many have done this very thing and led people astray. I will remind you again in Chapter 1. I encourage you to do this study with prayer, patience, and an open mind.

The chapters of this book are numbered identically with the chapters of the Book of Revelation. The verse by verse headings within the chapters will usually coincide with the paragraphs within a chapter of the Book of Revelation. This holds true if you are using *The Revised Standard Version, The New Revised Standard Version, Today's English Version, New International Version*, or *The Living Bible*. If you are using *The King James Version*, read the verse grouping and then read those verses in your Bible.

After reading the introductory chapters and Jesus' words from one of the Gospels, open this Reader's Guide to the corresponding chapter of the Book of Revelation. Beginning with chapter 1 read the Book of Revelation chapter by chapter or paragraph by paragraph and then read the comments in the Reader's Guide. Follow this procedure as you work your way through the complete book at least once. After that you can jump around or make reference to specific chapters or verses, always keeping in mind the importance of reading Scripture in its context of paragraph, chapter, and book.

Let God's Word speak to you and you will be blessed.

Introduction

What Is An Apocalypse?

Apocalypse is a Greek word. It is pronounced "a/pock/a/lips." The Latin translation of *apocalypse* is *revelation*. *Revelation* is then transferred from Latin into the English language, and thus we have the title of this book of the Bible. It sometimes helps our understanding if we say the Greek word is *apocalypse*, the Latin word is *revelation,* and the English word would be "unveiling." We could also loosely but accurately translate apocalypse as "vision."

Apocalyptic literature is a title given to a rather large group of writings, most of which were recorded between 200 B.C. and 150 A.D. Many of them were from the pens of Jewish authors, some from Christian authors, and others were Jewish writings with Christian additions. Since we have established that apocalypse can be loosely translated as "vision," it is obvious that some future thoughts or events are to be revealed in these writings. This same description could be applied to "prophecy," but there is a major difference.

Prophecy deals with earthly life and the future of present earthly history. An apocalypse goes beyond this earthly life to the promises of another existence. Prophecy encourages the unrepenting people to shape up, change, get with it, and return to God's ways. In an apocalypse the concern for the unrepentant is that they receive a judgment in accord with their lack of repentance. In simple thought, it is now too late to repent. The end has come.

The dates of this style of writing (200 B.C. - 150 A.D.) give a strong hint of its nature. The political conditions of this era were unstable and particularly discouraging to a renewal of the Jewish nation as a political entity. Only outside divine intervention could establish a Kingdom of God where righteousness would reign. The visions which developed out of this setting began to see history as a progressive plan which reached a final goal through the work of God.

With the coming of Jesus Christ (outside divine intervention) and the establishment of the "spiritual" Kingdom of God, or "the Kingdom of God among you" as Jesus refers to it, Christian apocalyptic writing looks beyond to the Second Coming of Christ and the final establishment of a permanent Kingdom where righteousness will always prevail. It is from this setting in history that we have received the Revelation of Jesus Christ to Saint John.

Understanding The Book Of Revelation

The Book of Revelation has been a puzzle to most of its readers. Martin Luther, for instance, wasn't really sure it belonged in the Bible. Pastors of mainline churches avoid preaching on its texts. Even when the church calendar lists the letters to the seven churches from chapters 2 and 3, pastors are more apt to preach on that Sunday's Gospel rather than "take a chance with Revelation." Because of the lack of understanding our curiosity is increased. Anyone who claims to offer insight is listened to, and his or her opinions are seldom questioned. Religious fanatics quote the Book of Revelation to support their warnings and prophets of doom use its passages as proof in explaining history or offering warnings.

The millennium brings forth the strangest of the strange. Back in A.D. 1000, before the advent of any form of mass communication (radio, television, printed books), prophets of doom and gloom arose and traveled wherever they could find an audience. The same phenomenon is happening as we approach A.D. 2000. This is not to say that there haven't been these prophets in other centuries. The millennium just seems to bring them out in greater numbers, which, coupled with anyone's curiosity about the unknown, will give them an audience.

The intriguing aspect of reaction to this book is that these avoidances, warnings, proofs, and frustrations have continued for centuries. When one date set for the end of the world is reached and then passed without a world catastrophe, another "prophet" arises to speculate on still another date. As far back as the sixteenth century, the astrologer Nostradamus predicted the demise of the world by the end of this twentieth century.

However, our age is the first to possess the tools of mass communication. From newspapers to facsimile machines, from cellular phones to pagers, from television to satellites, from e-mail to Internet, "the word" is passed from one person to the next without barrier of distance or time. We no longer just hear the news, we see the news. It's not just local, but worldwide. Troubles are not day-old history but on the scene, live, and happening now. Famine, war, pollution, and crime cannot be avoided. We cannot place ourselves into a void. And these are troubled times. Since the Book of Revelation grew out of a troubled era, it has best been understood in other troubled eras; and if we would describe our own era as troubled, this is indeed a book for today.

But that doesn't help our understanding. If anything we are more frustrated for not understanding it. **Therefore, let's slow down!** One cannot read this portion of scripture in a panic. Be patient! Be patient with this book and with yourself.

Over the years, we have not only had people preaching gloom and doom from this book, but we have people who claim to have a "method" or a "theory" that unlocks the meaning to this book. This thinking offers several problems. The first is that any method is just that, a method. Someone has devised it and someone must interpret how it works. That may sell books but it doesn't do justice to God's Word. Now you have superimposed a human method or theory upon God's Divine Word. That automatically limits God's Word. The Book of Revelation has much to offer us about God and God's attributes, God's people, God's plan, and God's promise. Let's let God's Word speak to us instead of our telling God's Word what it ought to be. Our God is a God of history and an ever-present God among us. We will understand this book as God gives us his grace to do so and as we open our hearts to hear it.

Characteristics Of The Book Of Revelation

While we cannot superimpose a theory upon this book, we can look at certain characteristics which are present in this type of writing. These characteristics are present in other books of the Bible and have stood the test of time in their use by both the sacred and the secular world.

Drama, symbols, and series are all a part of the Book of Revelation, and together they add to the uniqueness of this book. It's not that other literature doesn't make use of these devices, but rather it is the extensive use of these techniques that distinguishes apocalyptic literature from other forms of writing. We want to look for a minute at each of these devices individually in order to capture some of their importance in the writing of the Book of Revelation.

Drama: The Book of Revelation has many elements of drama present. The writer of this work or the one to whom Jesus unveils the message is not always just an observer or a reporter. There are times when the writer:

- turns to see a voice
- falls down
- is invited into heaven
- weeps
- is spoken to by a participant in the vision
- eats a scroll
- measures things
- is carried away by an angel

Scene: In addition to the drama, there are some who feel that the entire scene of chapters 4 and 5 is very similar to the arrangement of a Graeco-Roman theater. The fact that the author is invited up to something reminds us of going up on a stage. These theaters had a throne reserved for the emperor on the stage. The 24 thrones surrounding the main throne could have been like the box seats in the theater. The sea of glass separating the throne from the witness could depict the orchestra pit.

This idea has much validity. Whether or not it was the author's intention or inspired mood consciously to show this similarity is debatable, and the answer will never be known. However, it does show us the drama involved in bringing this revelation to the common people like first century Christians and like you and me.

Symbols: Symbolism is often spoken of as the language of apocalypse. It seems to be everywhere. Some of this symbolism has its origin in ancient mythology. We all know the importance of the sun and the stars in that belief. Other symbols that are used can be found in the Old Testament. Some of these are present in their completeness in the Book of Revelation, while others have been adapted and updated. Still other symbols are common to all of apocalyptic literature, including the Book of Revelation.

In the glossary of terms following this introduction, symbols are defined as "names, colors, numbers, animals, and figures whose meaning has greater significance than appears on the surface."

Even this definition is inadequate. Figures of speech sometimes defy definition. Today we may speak of someone's being "upbeat," "classy," or even "cool." We know we're not describing a conductor's baton or someone studying or another's body temperature. But will someone two thousand years from now know that? We might see a large diamond ring and describe the stone by saying, "It's as big as a baseball." What will someone think two thousand years from now?

Does a beast rising up out of the sea remind us of a large hairy animal or a foreign government? What is the significance of a rider on a certain color horse carrying a certain weapon, followed by a rider on another color horse with a different weapon?

This points up our difficulty with symbols. We can't be literal, but we want to know literally what the author meant.

There are names, numbers, colors, places, animals, and happenings in nature which have a different or greater meaning than a simple definition of the word. These will be considered as we progress through the reading guide.

Series: Everyone who reads or studies the Book of Revelation concludes that the number seven (7) plays a major part in the writing. Some scholars believe the book is consciously written in seven parts. Others believe it is like a seven-act play. The number occurs more than fifty times in Revelation's 22 chapters. This fact alone leads people to give special study to the number seven in the Book of Revelation.

But there are other numbers which are prominent in this writing. Twelve (12), four (4), three (3), and ten (10) are some of them. The phrase "time, times and half a time" adds up to three and a half times or three and a half years, so its equals become 42 months or 1260 days (based on a 360-day year). Is it significant that three and a half is just one-half of seven?

Numerology, the study of numbers as they influence one's life, is present in all apocalyptic writings, but it seems to be especially developed in this Revelation of Jesus Christ to Saint John. Astrologers in the immediate centuries before Christ regarded numbers as sacred. They had systems well enough developed that they were known by most people and borrowed by biblical writers.

• **Seven** was the perfect or complete number, because there were seven known planets comprising the complete universe. Think in how many days creation is described as taking place.

• **Twelve** was the number of signs in the Zodiac. But we also recognize twelve as the number of tribes of Israel. In the Old Testament these tribes are listed many different ways (i.e. one of Jacob's sons might be omitted and a grandson inserted), but there are always twelve listed. We also think of the twelve apostles. After Judas lost his place through betrayal and subsequent suicide, why couldn't they have operated just as well with eleven? Even when they decided to fill his spot, they found two good candidates: Justus and Matthias (Acts 1:21-26). If they were such equal candidates that lots had to be cast, why didn't they appoint both of them? Evidently twelve was felt to be their proper number.

• **Four** is very easily seen as the earthly number. The Psalmist refers to the four winds and the four corners of the earth. The earth was thought to be flat and square for centuries after Jesus walked the earth.

• **Three** is usually seen as a spiritual number. Through hindsight we can speak of the Trinity or three in one. The planets which intersected to cause a bright star in the East, leading wise men (astronomers) to Bethlehem, were three in number. There are three commandments from God that relate to humankind's relationship with God. The list could go on and on.

• **Ten** and **five** are related to travel. In Jesus' day, a ten-mile walk was a long walk or a day's journey, and a five-mile walk was one-half or a short walk.

Numbers are an important part of the series in Revelation. Since each series has seven parts, there are times when we easily see a division into four (the earthly number) and three (the spiritual number). We might add here that we can document more than seven churches in Asia Minor (from Paul's journeys), but the vision only speaks to seven.

The series of seven which are most prominent are: the letters to the churches, the seals, the trumpets, and the bowls. In each case there are seven of them. In some situations there is an interlude between the sixth and seventh happening. This is just part of the drama of the series. It's like a great symphony building to a climatic end, only to get very soft at the precise spot where we expected the cymbals to clash.

Much more time could be spent on the numbers and the series, but an absolute conclusion could not be reached on whether the book is built around the numbers or numbers are just part of the book. We can agree that they are important, but to go beyond that is to create a method or a theory, which we have dismissed as the placing of human thought on the Divine Word of God.

A Glossary Of Terms

Apocalypse	A Greek word which means the removal or unveiling of that which hides.
Dualism	A belief that life is a struggle between two great opposing powers.
Eschatology	The study of the last things, including the time before the end, the final judgment, and the resurrection to a new life.
Parousia	A Greek word which means "coming" or "advent." It is often used to describe the coming of Christ in glory to judge the world at the end of this age.
Proleptic	Anticipating the future with such certainty that its presence is already felt.
Prophecy	A prediction of a future *earthly* event.
Revelation	A Latin word used in the English language which means the removal or unveiling of that which hides. (see Apocalypse)
Symbols	Names, colors, numbers, animals, and figures whose meaning has greater significance than appears on the surface.
Vision	A special insight into the future through what is being seen by the seer or writer.

Chapter 1

Wait! Stop! It will only take a minute.

Please read Mark Chapter 13 before proceeding. (Matthew 24 and Luke 21 are also helpful in our preparation.)

It is very important that our discoveries, our insights, and our understanding of Revelation do not contradict Jesus' words to his followers about the end of time. Remember some of the signs in nature, the prediction of false Christs, the encouragement to be prepared, and the very important words which state that no one knows when the end will come. These were Jesus' own words, recorded by three different writers. They are in the Gospel which is central to our faith in Christ. Thank you for reading Mark 13. Now you can go on.

1:1-11

You have just begun reading one of the most frustrating and misused books of the Bible. These first eleven verses are pretty innocent and have caused no problems for readers, although scholars can debate for hours about the identity of John. Suffice it to say that most evidence points to John the apostle, brother of James, son of Zebedee. There was another John who was a church leader in Ephesus and to whom we attribute the epistles called 2 and 3 John in the New Testament. The only evidence pointing away from John the Apostle was a tradition that John and James, his brother, were killed by the Jews in 70 A.D. However, this is only a tradition with no factual evidence to back it up, so we'll stick with John the Apostle. We need to note some of the attributes of this writer:

• He had a broad knowledge of Jewish writings, as shown by the many quotes from the Old Testament.

• He knew very much about the churches in Asia Minor.

• Both writings (the Gospel of John and Revelation) have an imminent feel for the return of Christ.

• He shows a real pastoral concern for the church and Jesus' followers.

His broad knowledge of the Old Testament is shown by his quoting over two hundred passages from twenty different Old Testament writings. However, it is interesting that not one of his quotes is an identical word for word quote from the Old Testament.

The Revelation of Jesus Christ to Saint John (verse 1) It is extremely important always to remember this is Jesus' revelation to John. It is not something John is revealing, which would make it a human interpretation. It is Jesus' revelation or unveiling to John. So always emphasize the prepositions "of" and "to" when referring to the title.

John to the seven churches (verse 4ff) What beautiful opening words from John's pen as he witnesses to his faith in Jesus. "Who is and who was and who is to come" (verses 4 and 8) is a tremendous proclamation of the everlasting nature of the Lord Jesus Christ.

This paragraph is packed with great phrases referring to Jesus and the author's faith. It also alerts us to the future nature of this work, as verse 7 points to the Second Coming of Christ.

On Patmos, in the spirit, on the Lord's Day (verses 9, 10) What's John doing on this island? Patmos is located in the Aegean Sea approximately 55 miles southwest of Ephesus and 25 miles from the Asia Minor coast. He was there because of his testimony to faith in Christ. Patmos was a rocky island, known for its quarrying industry where prisoners placed on the island were required to work. It probably was like a prison farm would be today. It would house non-violent prisoners who had committed a variety of offenses. They would not be chained, but they couldn't give thought to escaping since it was an island 25 miles from shore.

"In the spirit" could mean many things. Maybe John was seated on a rock looking back toward the Asia Minor shore, thinking about the churches where he had been before his arrest. He could have been meditating on his faith in Jesus and the witness to Jesus which had gotten him arrested. He might have been doing something as simple as praying. It is interesting to note that the word "sea" occurs 25 times in the revelation. Here he was on an island, surrounded by the sea, meditating in some way on the Lord's Day.

Which day of the week this was (the Jewish Sabbath, the Christian Sunday, or even Easter Day) is of little significance. We don't want to argue for any particular day of the week, but we do want to point out that even in prison, John had found a way to worship on his designated day with the Lord.

From this setting he has every right to bring this message to the church. This man had declared his faith and, like his Master, was willing to suffer the consequences. He had gone through the persecution experience with which the young churches were now confronted.

The churches (verse 11) These seven churches are located on the Western end of Asia Minor. They are listed in the order in which a circuit rider or messenger would deliver the message, beginning with Ephesus and proceeding east, then south, and finally west again back to Ephesus. These are all real and historic churches which were begun under the preaching and work of Saint Paul some fifty years earlier.

1:12-16 *(The Christophany)*

The manifestation which John sees is strange but awesome. Here we are introduced to some of the symbolism of the Book of Revelation. Especially evident is the use of the number seven. We will see drama and symbols galore.

We said the author would become involved in this vision. He turns to see the voice and what he encounters is very startling. It's someone like "a son of man." These words are very reminiscent of Daniel 7:13 and 10:5. In fact, the scene along the river in the second of these passages is quite similar to John's being on an island and possibly looking across the water toward his home.

Let's look at the word picture. It is called a Christophany, which means a manifestation of Christ. There are two more of these in the revelation. From white hair to bronze feet with mouth, voice, eyes, breast, and face in between, we get a brilliant picture. If we look at this person according to the literal description, it is an impressive sight, but if we look at the symbolic significance, it is even more impressive. Even today we bronze shoes which have performed significant feats. They range from the shoes in which a baby took his first step to the mementos of bygone days which fill trophy cases in honor of most touchdowns made or new track records. They all signify victory. His victory was the greatest, and his feet were like burnished bronze.

His hair was so white it is described doubly. It is like white wool and snow. To this day we speak of someone with white hair as looking dignified. We also associate white hair with older age and increased wisdom.

The **voice** has an interesting quality. He wasn't gargling to "sound like many waters." The readers or hearers of this message, familiar with the prophets of old, would remember Ezekiel's vision of the temple and the glory of the Lord entering it.

> *And behold, the glory of the God of Israel came from the east; and the sound of his coming was like the sound of many waters; and the earth shone with the glory.* (Ezekiel 43:2)

So once again the glory of the Lord is seen. This time it is in John's vision of the person of Jesus Christ.

The **stars** in his hand (v. 16) are explained in verse 20 as angels. This can also be translated "messengers," which we could interpret as the leaders of the churches (which are in turn the lampstands). Oftentimes in this revelation, we need to be patient. Scripture can indeed interpret Scripture. And just a few lines after we are left scratching our head about the meaning, the writer explains exactly what it is. It is very reminiscent of how Jesus told the parable of the sower, the seed, and the soils.

A **sword,** the weapon of war which implies judgment, comes from his mouth. All war implies judgment because someone becomes an aggressor who believes he is either right in doing what he is doing or because he believes that he has been wronged. And that's judgment. The sword is not as important as the place from which it emanates, his mouth. It is not in his hand, it is in his mouth. When Jesus lived on earth, he judged with his words. The rich were not executed physically but *told* how difficult it would be to enter the Kingdom. The Pharisees were *verbally* scorned for their street corner prayer tactics.

The **lampstands** are the churches (v. 20). There are seven, so that means all the churches. But remember, the lampstands are lamp *stands*. The purpose of a lamp stand is to hold a lamp or a light. Christ is the light and he is in the midst of the lampstands (v. 13). We are sometimes guilty of believing that the church is an end unto itself when it is only a means. It is the place where the light shines and from which the light emanates, but the light is Christ.

In summary we can ask, "What does John see?" Does he see an old dignified man in hard shoes with a sword in his mouth? Or does he see the triumphant Christ who judges in wisdom, upholding his leaders and making his presence felt in the midst of his followers, the church? This points out to us the beauty and splendor of this revelation. The symbolic significance of the picture language so often used in that area of the world at that time reminds us that as humans we are limited by language and experience in describing and understanding divine happenings. We also live in a generation where everything is pictured for us on screens, so our imaginations are seldom used in the way they were created.

1:17-20 *(The One with the Keys)*

These manifestations are important to our study, but we must be careful not to miss the forest because of the trees. The description is meaningful and symbolic, but of prime importance is that this is the Christ. This is the one who gives the revelation. This is the one who instructs the author to write. This is the one who died and is alive forever (v. 18). This is the one with the keys to overcome death and the grave.

The result of this vision upon John is electrifying. He simply faints. I guess we would do the same if confronted by our Lord under similar circumstances. The drama of the vision is at work, and the author John is deeply involved. He isn't simply an observer of some historic event. He is a full participant in a spectacular revelation of what has been, what is, and what will be.

These are action-packed verses filled with descriptive references and strange ideas for human minds. It is not easy reading but it is exciting. It is also hope-filled. Right in this first chapter John sees and faints. Immediately the comforting hand of Christ reaches down and assures his follower of his identity, which is best known through the cross and resurrection.

There is an important message here for us as well. Never lose sight of the fact that Jesus Christ, son of God and son of man, is in the middle of all this. He is in the middle of our lives with the cross for our sins and the middle of our lives with the resurrection for our eternal hope. He strengthens, he upholds, he comforts, and he has the keys that open the door of the kingdom of heaven. He is constant in his love from age to age.

Points To Ponder

Whose revelation is this? And to whom was it given?

Where was John when he received this revelation and what was he doing?

How is Jesus Christ described in this chapter?

Chapter 2

Is this all there is sixty years after the resurrection and forty-five to fifty years since the beginning of Saint Paul's missionary journeys? Of course not! We are aware historically of the existence of some other congregations such as Hierapolis and Colossae. But remember that the church at this time was still small. It met in people's homes in various cities and each probably numbered between fifty to two hundred people, varying in size from place to place. Its size is one reason that we have begun to realize that the church was not persecuted as severely as once thought. Although the church refused to worship the emperor, it posed little threat to the empire. On the other hand, just one martyrdom from a small minority group like the Christians would be psychologically threatening to the remainder of the believers.

There are seven churches listed here. Seven symbolizes completeness. These seven then become examples to the whole church. The variety of their problems allows others to see themselves and their situations in the light of one of these seven.

These seven cities could also be listed because in most of them were found headquarters for the Imperial Cult. This was the title given to the form of worship which the people paid to the emperor. Emperor Domitian, during whose reign this book was written, was known to have demanded to be called "our Lord and God." Thus, these letters also serve as an introduction to the dualism of good and evil forces which is found throughout this work.

To hide from the evil forces of the Emperor, the symbolic language of this message could serve as an underground code language of a frightened and sometimes persecuted people. It would also explain how John could write such a message and have it sent from prison to the people. The government would have no idea about what he was writing. They had no Old Testament background and couldn't begin to understand the purpose and meaning of the church.

Chapters two and three are certainly part of the revelation, but the description of their problems and needs is not future directed toward another life. It applies right now to these actual congregations.

Form letters would be a good description of these seven letters. Their content differs, but the form or composition of each is almost identical. Some scholars have noted that even the form has seven parts. This is possible but it tends to overemphasize structure at the expense of the message. Here is what the letters have in common.

1. Location	Each congregation is identified by the city or town in which it is located.
2. Receiver	Each letter is addressed to the angel of that particular congregation. This probably means the deacon or leader.
3. Application	In each letter a portion of the Christophany in 1:12-16 is picked up and shown to the congregation as a symbol of authority under which the letter is sent.
4. Analysis	Each congregation has its own problems or unique situation.
5. Admonition	If the believers in a location have backslid they are admonished and if they have been strong they are encouraged.
6. Promise	Each one is given a reassurance of God who is constant in his love for his people. The rewards are reminders which reflect the Old Testament.
7. Motivation	Shape up, get with it, listen, hear!

The Christophany is played back. Piece by piece we can follow the reconstruction of the revealed Christ found in 1:12-16. The importance of this is vital. It points out the authorization under which the letter is sent, but it reemphasizes Christ in the midst of the lampstands (the churches). For instance, Ephesus hears the words (2:1) of the one holding seven stars and walking among the lampstands. Pergamum hears the words (2:12) of the one who has the sharp two-edged sword. Thyatira (2:18) hears the words of the

Son of God, who has eyes like flames of fire and feet like burnished bronze.

2:1-7 *(Ephesus)*

It is presumed by most scholars that Ephesus was the center of the churches in Asia Minor. In fact, it was probably the center of all Christianity after Jerusalem lost its influence. It was not the geographical center but the center of population and influence. Saint Paul visited this city on his second missionary journey (Acts 18:18-21) and left Priscilla and Aquila there to carry out the work. Later Paul returned and spent much time here. In Acts 19 we read about the important position which the temple of Artemis held in this city. This temple, begun in the sixth century B.C., was considered one of the wonders of the world, and many pilgrims came to worship at its shrine.

In addition to the time Priscilla and Aquila and Saint Paul spent in this city, John became the leader, and Timothy and Philip were also mentioned as having spent time here. This was indeed an important congregation.

To this congregation comes the words of the one who holds the seven stars and walks among the churches. The Ephesians have evidently kicked out some false teachers and remained strong in the face of threats from the surroundings of this heathen city. For this they are commended.

However, as often happens, when people remain firm in the midst of threat, they become hardened and no longer express love as they expressed it before the threat. The Ephesians are encouraged to return to that love.

The Nicolaitans are also mentioned. They were one of several groups within the early church which held opinions differing from the standard Christian beliefs and lifestyles which had developed. For this reason we refer to them as heresies. Differing views exist as to what this Nicolaitan heresy was. Some feel it had to do with eating meat sacrificed to idols. Others saw it as a sect which engaged in promiscuity. In either case, whether to purchase meat or to buy sexual favors, it would call for a visit to the temple of Artemis.

This temple was therefore seen as the prime threat to Christianity in Ephesus.

The promise for repenting is symbolically beautiful and filled with hope. This book holds much hope for the strong believers.

2:8-11 ***(Smyrna)***

Here is a letter of encouragement to a church which is poor financially. In another environment this might not have mattered, but Smyrna was a coastal town with a good harbor. It was a trade center and as such a wealthy city.

In addition there seems to have been persecution against these Christians (v. 9). Smyrna had always been loyal to Rome and had been the first city to erect a temple to the goddess Roma.

In this city the Jews were quite numerous and influential. The Christian church probably drew its converts from this group, and these converts in turn were persecuted and ostracized for their conversion. No wonder the opposition is called a Synagogue of Satan.

But the worst is yet to come (v. 10). It always seems that people who are already down get hit the hardest. This was certainly true in Smyrna.

On the other hand, nothing compares to the promise of faithfulness, the crown of life. In addition, the faithful are unhurt by "the second death." This phrase is a common expression in the biblical writings which alludes to the separation from God in eternity following an earthly death.

2:12-17 ***(Pergamum)***

To this congregation come the words of Christ who is the concerned judge of all humanity. Pergamum had an identity all its own. It was not a seaport (some fifteen miles inland), nor was it located on the great highways, but it was still the capital city of the Roman province of Asia. Built high on a hill, it offered a magnificent view of the surrounding area. It was also the center of culture and the home of many temples, including the altar of Zeus and a temple to the goddess Roma. Many pilgrims visited this city and its temples. Here the church faced conflict with the historic religion of the Greek gods.

The Christians of Pergamum are commended for their faithfulness, evidently even at the cost of the life of one of their fellow believers. Two heresies seemed to have crept into this church.

The first concerned the tradition of Balaam. The Old Testament book of Numbers (chapters 22-24) relates to us the story of Balaam who prophesied Israel's triumph over the Moabites. Legend developed that Balaam would have cursed the King of Moab if he could have. With this cunning personality trait as a starter, numerous stories developed concerning Balaam's teaching of immoralities.

Coupling the first heresy with that of the Nicolaitans, these teachings show us that the believers in Pergamum were slipping in their morality. They are warned to repent, and if they do they will receive the hidden manna. This shows how they were looking in the wrong places for their sustenance. The white stone symbolizes membership. In this center of culture and gods there were many membership groups with their individual identifications. The promise is for a special group with an identification known only to God.

2:18-29 *(Thyatira)*

The triumphant Christ with discerning eyes is brought to bear upon the church in Thyatira. This is the longest of the seven letters, yet Thyatira held little importance other than being the gateway to Pergamum. This leads us to think that her problems were common problems facing the church of that day.

Jezebel, another Old Testament personage, is used to describe their problem. Evidently a seductive female teacher was in their midst. The people had become indifferent to the disciplines of life and allowed her to lead them into the same sins we found affecting Pergamum. The message of this letter is sobering. The sin (v. 22) will create its own punishment.

The reward for the faithful is strange. The "rod of iron" type of rule is unfamiliar teaching in a promised spiritual kingdom. "The morning star" of verse 28, which suggests freshness and newness, is more appropriate.

Points To Ponder

How are the churches described and are there churches like these today?

How would you feel if your church was receiving this letter?

Chapter 3

3:1-6 *(Sardis)*

Once again the Christ, who holds the leaders and is present among the churches, speaks his word to this particular church.

Hundreds of years before the writing of this letter, Sardis was the wealthy capital of Lydia, an empire of that time. Wars, coupled with the feeling that the city was impregnable, led to its downfall under King Croesus. Still a city of merchant wealth, this was threatened by an earthquake in A.D. 17. Rebuilt through the generosity of the Roman Emperor, Sardis had some semblance of wealth even in John's day, but its end was inevitable.

The young Christian fellowship in this town fit the pattern of the city. The revelation does not find even a small reason for commendation of the congregation as a whole. This church has only a reputation for being alive, when in reality it is dead. In the midst of the promise of coming like a thief in the night, a few individuals are singled out for remaining firm. They receive the promise of having their names in the book of life.

3:7-13 *(Philadelphia)*

In direct contrast to Sardis is Philadelphia. Philadelphia was a young town, a little over two hundred years old, founded for the purpose of spreading Greek culture eastward. This city was affected by the same earthquake as Sardis in A.D. 17. History tells us that this city was thankful for Rome's help in rebuilding and twice changed its name to honor the family name of emperors.

This church receives all praise from the one with the keys. It too, like Smyrna, has as its opponent the Synagogue of Satan. Evidently there was no strong government opposition or repression, but trouble came from the Jews, among whom no doubt most Christian converts were made.

Many people have called this a missionary church because of the "open door" phrase (v. 8). Our text is not clear on this, but it is safe to say that its location, lack of suppression, and its Christian spirit gave it the potential for missionary spirit.

An Old Testament picture is once more found in the promise of "a pillar in the temple of God."

3:14-22 *(Laodicea)*

The seven-church journey of the revelation ends its circular route at the southern end, in the city of Laodicea. Laodicea was one of the major trade routes between Ephesus and the East and was the home of a great Roman medical school.

Like Sardis there are no words of praise for the church in this city. The problem is obvious. The city's wealth is also found in the church, and along with its financial independence come spiritual complacency and indifference. The church is admonished (v. 18) to seek the correct wealth for their spiritual poverty.

Verse 20 is a famous quote of assurance to any remnant which might be present, and the promise of sitting on the throne is most fitting in this Roman Empire where all these churches were located.

Summary

Many people have done many things with these two chapters. Some have seen them as depicting seven different historical eras of the church. In this way it is easy to show a decline in the church from Ephesus to Laodicea. Suffice it to say that these seven all existed at the time of John's vision. Their historic descriptions are well substantiated outside of scripture. And the church has had enough ups and downs in nearly 2,000 years to go though this cycle of seven at least ten times.

The problems which were present in these particular churches are typical of many which have arisen throughout history. Some of them are even familiar to us in the church today. Such things as people using the church for selfish gain or the lukewarm commitment of members are well known and often experienced in the American church. On the other hand, we know of strong commitment by some Christians who live under totalitarian rule. God's promises and warnings are the same for Christians today as they were for the Ephesians, Smyrnans, Thyatirans, and so forth.

This is the message for today. Christ is in the midst of the church, concerned and hopeful of continued repentance. To follow this Christ is to chance persecution, sometimes physical and sometimes verbal. But no matter how hard times become, the promise is sure. God through Christ is constant in his love, and the great promise must focus on an expectation of Christ's return.

Points To Ponder

What is the promise that you find in these letters?

Did you pick out a favorite church among the letters? Why that one?

Where is Jesus Christ in these letters?

Chapter 4

From the earthly problems and weak human commitment of chapters 2 and 3, we turn dramatically to the next two chapters to see a heavenly scene. This change is a further reminder of the drama involved in apocalyptic literature.

There is much dramatic involvement for the seer in these verses. In 4:1, John looks, hears, and is even invited up.

Symbolism abounds in these chapters. Not only does the number seven appear repeatedly, but four, six, and twelve are also found here. We can recall from the introduction some of their significance.

- 4 The earthly number.
- 6 (a new one) Just a little less than 7, which is perfect. Therefore six is the human number, since humans were created perfect and then fell into imperfection through sin.
- 12 The number of the elect.

This **scene** is one of joy and worship. The picture is scary, mysterious, awesome, and comforting, all rolled into one. The rainbow and white robes remind us of victory, and the thunder, lightning, and fire are symbolic of judgment.

Since hope for the believers under persecution is one of the themes of this revelation, chapters 4 and 5 provide them with some wonderful assurances. In chapters 2 and 3 we had a picture of a small, persecuted church being bombarded by numerous threats from without and heresies from within. Things did not look good. One church is warned that the worst is yet to come. Now we find in chapter 4 a promise of better things to come. There is hope in the midst of a troubled church to give honor, glory, and thanks without interruption.

4:1-6 ***(The Throne Scene)***

The seer is taken up to view this worship of God which is taking place. The scene is reminiscent of the setting for a Graeco-

Roman theater. These amphitheaters were often built into a hillside for seating. They would often have a throne for the emperor at the back edge of the stage. The seer reveals at the end of verse 2 that there was one seated on the throne. The 24 thrones surrounding the main throne remind us of the special box seats for important people which were located just beyond the orchestra pit. The importance of all this is that it shows pictures which the readers in John's day would have recognized. This was not a frustrating scene without any meaning but was a familiar sight with added beauty.

We have many symbolic elements in these verses, ranging from the white robes (of victory), the golden crowns (reigning), the lightning and thunder (judgment), and the sea of glass. This sea, as any sea, would provide separation. But this sea was like a sea *of glass*, which is transparent and therefore would not hinder the seer's view. He could see the action which was taking place.

4:6-11 *(The Creatures and The Elders)*

There are four living creatures on each side of the throne. Four is the earthly number (like the four corners of the earth), and the fact that these creatures surround the altar on all sides further emphasizes their representation of the whole earth. They are not a lion, ox, eagle, or face of a man, but are *like* these creatures; that is, they have their attributes. The stealth of a lion, the loyal hard work of an ox, the soaring flight of an eagle, and the intelligence portrayed by the face of a man heighten the drama and increase the greatness of the scene. The songs that they sing are the most important message of these verses. The emphasis in this section is placed on the eternal greatness of God. The song is one of continual (day and night) praise and thanks to the one "who was and is and is to come!" (v. 8). The song reminds us of the vision of Isaiah 6:1-3. Even the six-winged seraphim are carried over into the wings of the creatures who are singing in Revelation. We are further reminded of our own Trinitarian hymn of praise which no doubt was inspired by both of these visions: "Holy, Holy, Holy, Lord God Almighty."

Points To Ponder

Is this a happy or a sad scene? Strange or familiar?

What was the spirit of the song which was being sung?

Can you remember what some of the numbers were symbolic of? (4, 6, 7, 12)

Chapter 5

5:1-5 *(The Scroll)*

Remembering that this is still a portion of the heavenly vision, we next encounter the scroll. A scroll was a very important item to the people of the Roman Empire. Their destiny was guided by scrolls. The edicts of the empire were contained in scrolls carried by messengers who traveled from city to city. The scroll was the governmentally controlled television, radio, and newspaper all rolled into one. The people's future was in the scroll.

This scroll was no different. It was viewed as a message of destiny. But there was something unique about it. Sealed completely with seven seals (note the symbolism), no one could open it. A strong angel cries out for someone worthy to open it. John, the seer, gets so involved that he weeps (v. 4). Who can open it? The "Lion and the Root" can!

This is very dramatic. The feeling expressed provides an emotion with which all Christians can easily identify. The scroll's significance has already been discussed above. The believers know that something important and pertaining to them is contained within the completely sealed scroll. Everyone wants to know what is in it.

The message of this section is pretty obvious. We cannot join that scene by ourselves. No one is worthy. We are certainly not worthy. Just when things are looking really bad, one of the elders says, "Wait, there is someone!" There is someone who has conquered and that makes him worthy to open it.

Now we could ask why the seer just didn't come right out and say Jesus Christ can do it. Remember the church is suspect at this time, subject to persecution. John is in exile, in prison. Someone has to carry this message to someone else. Somewhere along the line government officials had to be involved. Disguised language like this looked harmless to officials but brought hope to the believer.

Jesus has conquered. He holds the keys. He can open the scroll. The future will be known.

5:6-14 ***(The Lamb)***

Now we see sets of almost impossible opposites. The seer looks around for a lion and spots a lamb. To top it all off, this lamb is "standing as though it had been slain or slaughtered." This is another example of how a literal reading of words only baffles us and misses the point.

The Lamb, of course, is Christ, and the fact that he was slain (sacrificed) is what makes him strong to stand, and qualified to open the scroll. This animal is probably the most important figure in the Book of Revelation. Only the wisdom of God could choose this sacrificial animal as a symbol of strength. We note (v. 6) that the lamb had seven horns and seven eyes, complete perfection in every way. That the lamb is worthy (v. 12) to open the scroll is a highly significant item. Remember, verse 3 stated that no one could be found to open it. Now we not only find someone to open it, but that someone is worthy. And that someone is depicted as a lamb. We cannot help recalling the words of John the Baptist, who declared, "Behold, the Lamb of God, who takes away the sin of the world" (John 1:29).

The seer has depicted a glorious scene indeed. It weaves the creatures and the elders back into the picture with a new song. This song is so great that thousands of angels now lend their voices to the praise of the Lamb.

The theology of this section is crucial to the believer. The one who is worthy is depicted as the lowly lamb, the sacrificial animal of the Old Testament. It is important that we remember over and over again that it was the lamb's sacrifice which made him worthy (5:6, 12).

The ascription of praise (5:12) is sevenfold. We once again see the book revolving around that number. Coupled with that (5:13) is a fourfold praise from four places. How much we want to dwell on the numbers and how much John's first readers understood about these numbers is debatable. Yet the message is obvious. It is the constant love of God for his people that caused the Lamb to be slain and now stand worthy to open the scroll. In response to this love, like the elders, creatures, and angels, we should sing praise forever and ever.

So the worship scene ends as it began with the living creatures praising the one on the throne and the lamb. Think of the hope this brought to a downtrodden, loosely organized, ill-equipped group of believers.

Yes, yes, yes, there is a forever.

Points To Ponder

Why was the scroll so important?

Why is the lamb so worthy to open it?

What were some of the traits of the lamb?

Chapter 6

Introduction ***(The Series of Seals)***

This chapter could be described as the beginning of the judgments in Revelation. A question can be raised as to how many judgments there are. There is one final judgment, but many partial judgments leading up to the final one. The series of seven seals is one of these partial judgments. The reason why it is only partial will become obvious as you read the verses. Since the scroll is a symbol of destiny it should not surprise us that the opening of the seals brings forth judgment.

One cannot read this chapter in isolation. Even though the scenes change from chapter to chapter in a very dramatic way, the Revelation of Jesus Christ to Saint John builds and relates the various scenes to one another. The movement goes from the mundane reality of congregations on earth in chapters 2 and 3 to the reassuring scene of God and Christ in chapters 4 and 5 and now back to the mundane of the earth again. Separated, these scenes are just scenes, but taken as a whole we find the promise of God's love for his people (chapters 4 and 5) includes an awareness of what is happening in the church (chapters 2 and 3) and God's active hand in what will be happening in the future (chapters 6 and following).

Judgment is a reoccurring theme in Revelation. The God of power and might with the ability to show his love by becoming one of us in history, then dying and rising, also has the ability to continue to be active in history. Historically, the majority of people have turned their backs to this love. Others have been receptive to this love and have loved in return. They show love to God and to their fellow humans. He cares for them and gives promises and assurances. The picture of the Worship Scene (chapters 4 and 5) is a promise of similar joy and praise at the resurrection to a new earth merged with heaven for those who believe. The judgment of God undergirds this promise.

There is also judgment for those who turn their backs to God. The judgment may take one of two forms.

First, as shown in this chapter, judgment may be brought upon people by their own actions. If we do not love, which implies reaching out, we turn in. We turn in to ourselves, and the attributes of our lives quite naturally become selfishness, greed, and hostility. These attributes collectively lead to hate and war. These are harmful attributes which cause suffering and death. These results are judgments which God has allowed to happen, but which are caused by the people themselves.

The second form of judgment in history is divine intervention. Apocalyptically, this is often pictured in the forms of happenings in nature.

The results of these two types of judgment are initially partial and eventually complete. When this judgment is seen as complete it is the final judgment. This will be discussed in detail when we reach those chapters which describe its finality in a variety of ways.

6:1-8 *(The Four Horsemen)*

These verses are jam-packed with symbolism. Each horse is a different color. Each rider has a different weapon. Each one goes forth with a purpose. And all are interrelated. For now we'll discuss the horses first.

Just as numbers are symbolic, so are colors. Most of these colors have maintained their meaning until today.

- White reminds us of victory.
- Red reminds us of bloodshed.
- Black reminds us of famine.
- Pale or colorless reminds us of death.

The white horse comes out first. Its purpose is to conquer. White may stand for victory, but apocalyptic symbolism is not consistent as to whether this is victory for good or for evil. In this case it is evil, because it is followed by bloodshed (red), famine (black), and death (pale).

As the second seal is opened, a bright red horse emerges. Red is the color of blood. Bloodshed which follows someone going forth to conquer means just one thing, war.

Think again about this progression as we move to the third horse. First is the one who goes to conquer. This means war develops. If war develops, someone must fight. This calls for all able-bodied men to take up arms. If they take up arms, there are few left to tend the crops, and famine naturally follows. This is depicted in the third seal as a black horse emerges. Its meaning is further emphasized by the fact that the rider carries a balance.

If conquering leads to war, and war to famine, death cannot be far behind. The fourth seal opens and a pale horse emerges. The translation here is really "colorless" or "transparent." In any case the rider's name is Death.

This picture should have been very familiar to its readers. The Roman Empire in which they lived was powerful but unsteady. The people of Asia Minor had experienced a Roman-Parthian battle in A.D. 60, the destruction of Jerusalem in A.D. 70 and its resultant persecution of Christians, and the bitter infighting of four potential emperors following Nero's death, as well as many local struggles for power.

Some scholars see the bow which the first rider carries as symbolizing the conquest of the Parthians. They were the only warriors of that time who used the weapon. With that idea, these verses warn of an invasion from the East. It is no doubt a possibility. In a larger context it seems more important that this bow symbol is a contrast with the victory of Christ. The war symbol of God is always the sword. The Christophanies of Revelation 1:12-16 and 19:11-16 typify God's symbolic use of weaponry. With this understanding, the message it reveals is that the warring conquest by people brings judgment upon itself. The real concern then is not who this is, but what happens.

The significance of the third horseman is interesting. We said it symbolized famine. This is obvious in both the facts that the rider carries a scale on which to weigh things and that it costs that day's average wage (a denarius) for an average day's basic food (a quart of wheat). In addition, the oil and wine would not be touched. Oil and wine were luxury items. It is the basic necessities which cause famine. People can live either with or without the luxury items, but they face famine when the necessities become scarce.

To summarize these eight verses, let's go back to the first verse. The Lamb opens the seals, but it is one of the living creatures who calls forth each horse. The fact that this is a living creature emphasizes that judgment is being pronounced upon the earth. Revelation 6:8 shows their power over "a fourth of the earth." That's a large amount, but it is still only a partial judgment.

6:9-11 *(The Martyred Saints)*

Another seal is opened, and the seer sees the souls (a word sometimes meaning persons) of those who died because of the word of God. These are martyrs who had been killed for witnessing to God. They cried out for vengeance, which is only natural after what they had been through. The promise from God to uphold those who trust in him is shown by the martyrs' placement under the altar. The altar is symbolic of God's presence, and the position under the altar is symbolic of God's protection.

Literally this picture could give the idea of a conscious existence after death as we await eternal life on the new earth. This points out to us the danger of a literal understanding of the revelation. Biblically, humankind is revealed as a unity. We have a body into which God has breathed spirit (potential for life). At death the body goes to the grave and the potential is gone. In biblical words we say "the spirit returns to God who gave it" (Ecclesiastes 12:7). That the period of time between earthly death and eternal life is an unconscious time is depicted by the illustration of sleeping. This is further developed by the description of the time lapse as being like "the twinkling of an eye" (1 Corinthians 15:52).

So what is really happening in verses 9-11? It is a vision of assurance that God is constant in his care for those whom he loves. The crying out of the martyrs shows how bad the situation is on the earth. It also shows our natural reaction when we are persecuted.

The beauty of symbolism is that it makes the picture bigger. It takes on meaning for us today. It doesn't dwell on the who but rather on the what. It is no longer a picture of ghostly figures screaming from the inside of a three-foot by six-foot structure called an altar at the front of a church, but is a picture with the message for us that, when we are true to the faith, God will be constant in his care for us, even during the time between earthly death and eternal life.

So these verses become another sign of hope to the believer. When things are bad, and personal life is in danger, the constant love of God cares for his people. Even those already killed for their faith are not forgotten by God.

6:12-17 *(The Wrath of the Lamb)*

In marked contrast to the judgment which people bring upon themselves as shown by the four horsemen, the sixth seal is opened to reveal a happening in nature. Again the real fear of such a happening was known to John's readers through a series of devastating earthquakes some thirty years prior and the very recent eruption of Mount Vesuvius in A.D. 92.

The message of all this is its cause. Verse 16 points back to our figures of chapters 4 and 5, the one on the throne and the Lamb. The power of God is great, and its strength is shown in his wrath as well as his love. When we concentrate so long and hard on the love, grace, and mercy of God, we tend to forget that the very power which makes that love and grace actual to us can be used in judgment against those who reject it. The power of nature is so devastating that people hide in the mountains and ask for them to cave in.

So we learn that when mankind turns away from God, he can expect either self-judgment or divine intervention and sometimes both. This should not strike fear in the hearts of believers, but should remind us to renew our commitment to God by saying yes every day to his love for us.

Keep in mind now all that you have read. We are now into the heart of the book. The historic letters are behind us, the vision of worship has prepared us, and now the future unfolds. That future may include self-destruction through war and a divine warning for those who fail to turn to God. On the other hand, the faithful who have "died for the cause" are safe under the altar of God. So keep asking what the message was to the people of John's day and what the message is for us today. We can see the images of horses, souls, and the Lamb and say, "So what?" But if we hear the message of God as relevant right now, we must either answer yes or no.

Points To Ponder

Can you remember the color of the horses and what these colors represented?

Where were the saints and why were they there?

Have you had any experiences as frightening as the earthquake of this chapter?

Chapter 7

This is an **interlude**, a scene filled with hope for the believer. In the midst of judgment humankind brings upon himself and judgment God himself gives, there is promise for the faithful. Will I be one of the select few? No! You will be one of the select many. Judgment will continue, but you have God's promise to the faithful.

The interlude is very important to our understanding. It is a dramatic device that will be used again in other series. The first six seals have been opened. The destiny of humankind looks bad. Wars and natural devastation surround it. We know there are seven seals and we expect the worst blow to come at any moment when the seventh seal is opened. We brace for the big climax. But like a great symphony, the revelation has a peaceful interlude before the climax. This happens in all of our series of sevens: the seals, the trumpets, and the bowls. In this, chapter 7 constitutes the interlude before the seventh seal is opened in 8:1. The interlude is very much a part of the series and constitutes some of the most necessary verses in all of the book.

7:1-3 *(The Angels)*

An angel is a messenger of God. All gods in John's day had their servants, and our God is no exception. What they were like and how they looked are questions that logical, analytical, mathematical Western minds would ask. The people in that time and geographical area of the world where the Bible was written did not concern themselves with this type of question. They probably never thought of it, because they didn't think in that way. Their language was a descriptive picture language with a message. In the previous chapter we might have wondered how big and what kind the horses were. The Mediterranean mind simply asked what this meant. Thus when we see angels in the revelation we should not worry about their looks or how they came to be, but rather we should wonder about their purpose.

In this section the angels show us that God is at work on the earth in this history. The picturesque language has the angels holding back the four winds. The number four emphasizes the earth. If we get literal with this picture it looks silly, but when we see its message of God working to save his people through supernatural means we begin to understand.

The sealing (v. 3, and repeated in v. 4) is an interesting concept. The seal was a mark of ownership in John's day. In this case, God was placing his seal of ownership upon the redeemed. That it was "on the forehead" in plain sight simply added to the realism. It is no secret. You are God's. This is your promise.

7:4-10 *(144,000 and the Multitude)*

With the wrath of the Lamb showering down on the unbeliever, the person who belongs to God is apt to ask, "Where do I fit in?" This is where: the wrath is momentarily held back until the servants of God are accounted for (v. 3).

Now we read the number that has troubled people, started sect groups, and maybe led more people to try to read this book than any other phrase found within it. The number 144,000 of verse 4, whether symbolic or literal, must be read in the same breath with the great multitude of verse 9. Many reasons for this dual listing have been proposed through the years. Some have said the 144,000 is the number of martyrs, and the multitude takes care of the rest. Some have said 144,000 is the number of Jewish converts to Christianity and the multitude covers the Gentile Christians. One sect group says the 144,000 will reign with God and the multitude covers the rest of the saved. Still others have seen this number as totally symbolic since 144 is the square of 12 and multiplied by 10 cubed equals 144,000. Here it would have the same significance as Jesus' seventy times seven statement of Matthew 18:22.

How did the Christians of John's day understand this? To a congregation which numbered its membership in the hundreds at best, and to whom a day's journey was about ten miles, 144,000 was a very big number. There had to be assurance to the believer simply in the size of this number. Christians must have been excited by its mention.

Twelve, of course, is the complete number. There are many different listings of the tribes of Israel in scripture, but there are always twelve. This listing is different from any other in scripture. Again many ideas are forthcoming as to why, but let us simply be satisfied with the completeness and the size offered here.

144,000 must be seen in connection with a multitude which no man could number. To do otherwise is to pull a verse out of its context. So the conclusion must be that these numbers constitute a great assurance of God's love and grace for those who trust in him.

The multitude from every nation, tribe, people, and tongue would provide an equally assuring promise to the Gentiles. Note the use of four in this listing (nation, people, tribe, tongue). This symbolizes the whole earth from which these people would come. The exact number of the saved or sealed would have caused little worry to the reader. That there were many and that they were among them is the promise.

The promise is then beautifully underlined with the white robes and palm branches (7:9). These symbols of victory are worn and carried as the faithful give credit where credit is due (v. 10).

7:11-17 *(A Worship Scene)*

A delightful scene pulling in the figures of the worship sequence in chapters 4 and 5 follows. This shows how Revelation is one book. We can't take a verse here and a verse there to satisfy our needs or method. The book is a whole, wherein the parts of previous chapters are woven back into the present scene time and time again. The interrelation is obvious and the divine inspiration of this message reaches out to us in all its glory.

Note the ascription of praise (7:12). There are seven words after the Amen. Amen means "so be it" or "this is true," and that amen is followed by a complete (seven) praising of God.

But where is this and what's going on? Where have the "sealed ones" been taken? To heaven is a simple answer, and now we revisit the throne scene of chapters 4 and 5 with all of its auxiliary beings: the elders, the angels, and the creatures. This is proleptic and visionary. John himself is there, as evidenced by his carrying on a conversation with an elder. We call it proleptic because to see it as actual would conflict with the fact that John and his readers were still on earth. By proleptic, we mean an anticipation of something in the future which becomes so real that it seems already to have arrived. John really gets involved here. He is even asked a question by that elder. It may be a vision, but it is so real to John that he sees himself right in it. When asked to identify the people, John turns the question back upon the elder as kind of a double check that he is really seeing what he thinks he sees.

That they have come out of great tribulation would be very meaningful both to John and his readers. They knew tribulation, they sometimes questioned the worth of their involvement, and they were known for having grown weak, weary, or complacent at times (chapters 2 and 3). Yet this is a promise. They are sheltered by God, know not hunger, thirst, nor tears, and are guided to living water by the Lamb, their Shepherd. This is a beautiful but literally impossible picture. Have you ever seen a lamb shepherding a flock of sheep? Think about that! Only the greatness and wonder of God could make this so.

And who are the ones being guided? It is another impossible picture. Those who wash robes *white* in the *blood* of the Lamb. How does something washed in blood become white? What a picture! Humanly and logically an impossible scene, but symbolically filled with great meaning. The eternal truth is that the Son of God (the Lamb) died for the sins of humankind and then shepherds them forever. And we conclude by saying "if they follow."

Points To Ponder

What is an angel? Have you ever experienced one?

How many were saved? Think hard.

How were the robes made white?

Chapter 8

8:1-5 *(The Seventh Seal)*

When the seventh seal is opened, there is silence. Not for very long, only a half-hour. But when you are waiting for the final blow, it can seem terribly long. This is dramatic. Suspense builds. What's next? We're ready for the climax, the great judgment. But wait, there is another dramatic device.

The seventh seal opens, and flashing onto the screen are seven trumpets. Like life, just when one task is almost completed, the next one begins. The series all tie together. They are separate but also parts of the whole. To emphasize this, the next series flows out of the previous one. So be prepared for the seven trumpets. And who gets to blow the trumpets? Why it's God's messengers or angels.

Once again we are confronted with happenings in nature as evidence of divine judgment. The censer is thrown upon the earth to show us where the next action will be. The censer, which held the incense and gave off smoke, had a dual purpose. It points out the prayers of the saints and then is thrown down amid some scary happenings in nature. The picture is filled with fear and awe. It is a picture of assurance to the faithful and of warning to the faithless.

We can't emphasize enough that this section be seen as an assuring scene for the believer. There is hope, expectation, and promise all wrapped together.

Introduction *(The Series of Seven Trumpets)*

We turn from the seals to the trumpets. We are still concerned with judgment. With the seals we learned that people bring judgment upon themselves and that happenings in nature are a warning of the divine judgment which is continually present in history.

One should not see these chapters as an historical progression of judgments which follow each other in a neat and clean chronological sort of way. Rather we should realize that both of these types of judgment can be taking place simultaneously. There are not reasons which cause people's judgment to be brought upon themselves and reasons which cause God to judge. There is really only one reason, sin, and mankind has made both of these types of judgment inevitable.

It would be good to pause here in our reading and remember as we read to look for the big truths such as the power of God, hope and assurance for the believer, and the unrepentance of the unbelievers. As we view the trumpets it can also be helpful to read the account of the plagues of Egypt in Exodus 7-11. They are not identical but have much in common. This further emphasizes the constant love of God for his people throughout the history of humankind.

8:6-12 *(The First Four Trumpets)*

The judgments brought in by the first four trumpets are all partial in nature. Each of them affects the earthly people in some way. A list of things affected would look like this.

Trumpet	Agent	Where	Effect
first	hail and fire	earth	vegetation
second	mountain (volcano)	sea	commerce
third	great star	rivers	drinking water
fourth	eclipse	sky	light

Some have said there is no evangelism in the Book of Revelation. I may even have inferred that when I discussed prophecy versus apocalypse. In the sense of an outward sharing of the love of Christ, this is true. There is no direct teaching. But indirectly there is a great call to repentance. Whenever there are wars and strange happenings in nature, people have turned back to God. Even today the discovery that we are not in control of everything shakes us to our senses.

Looking at the first four trumpets we see hail, a volcano, a meteor, and an eclipse. Look at the way they are introduced by the censer with thunder, noise, lightning, and an earthquake. Prophets of doom have spoken out in our lifetime regarding disturbances in the sun, moon, and stars as being signs of the end. Some groups even run to the mountains or hide within the mountains in caves. Basically we have to agree with these doom prophets. These are signs of the end. **But**, *every* peal of thunder, flash of lightning, earthquake, comet, volcano, and eclipse since the beginning of time is a sign. It is a sign of the end in that all of earthly life moves toward an end. It is not a sign of when it is going to happen. "But of that day and hour no one knows ..." (Matthew 24:36a). Earthly speaking, these are signs, reminders, or warnings that humankind is never in total control. God is ever present among us, and we are called to repent and turn to him in trust. To the persons who trust, there should not be fear but reassurance. The fact that these happenings are ushered in by the blowing of trumpets is a symbol of calling attention. Attention is called to the power of God and that there is still time to repent.

These first four trumpets have blown in some real fear-striking happenings in nature. But please note that the results of these happenings are *partial* destructions of earth, trees, sea, rivers, sun, moon, and stars. One peculiar item stands out in this partial destruction. Revelation 8:7 mentions one-third of earth and trees, but *"all the grass"* is burnt up. No one can read the mind of the writer or the revealer's thoughts. "*All* the grass" just doesn't seem to fit when everything else is one-third. It will just have to be one of those mysteries, the answer to which we do not know. With all the other one-thirds, we can still safely say that destruction is partial.

Let's look just a little deeper at the effects of the destruction. All of the actions have an effect upon humankind. The portion of the earth which is burned obviously makes that part uninhabitable. Traveling through any area which has suffered a forest fire brings this point home. Not only are the trees burned with all their seeds which attract birds or produce fruits which people eat, but the heat of a fire drives the life out of the topsoil and makes it untillable for decades until the humus of dying vegetation (weeds, leaves, etc.) builds the soil back up to usable standards.

The effect of the volcano spewing lava into the sea not only kills sea creatures but ruins parts of the merchant fleets on which many people's livelihood depend.

At first glance it seems strange that both sea and rivers should be mentioned, but the effect upon the sea is commercial shutdown and upon the river is undrinkable water. The word "wormwood" is found in the Book of Jeremiah. There, however, it is not used as a proper name but rather as a word for a bitter herb. The effect there is the same, in that the waters become poisoned.

The strange occurrences in the sun, moon, and stars brought in by the four trumpets obviously would baffle people, make them physically cold, and provide a very gloomy world.

Now the **big** question. Has this happened or will it ever happen? Maybe a better question is can this happen? If we believe in the power of God as being greater than anything, then we must also confess, yes, it can happen.

Has it ever happened? Literally, no! Symbolically, yes. Many happenings in nature have affected people throughout many ages. We must also add that the known world in John's day was much smaller geographically than we think of the world today. An eruption of Vesuvius with its terrible consequences could be considered by its survivors to have wiped out a significant portion of their environment. Or in our day, think of the pollution of our waters. Certainly it hasn't been instantaneous, and it has been caused by ourselves, but its effect could be consequential for millions.

Will it ever happen? It matters not. The warning is there. The message is clear. The results have already been seen by us in small ways. If we are approaching this book symbolically in most other areas, this area should be no different. Remember that the message is our most important concern, and in this case the message had meaning then and it also has meaning now.

These warnings can be added to the wars, famines, earthquakes, comets, thunder, lightning, and other happenings in nature which remind us that our God is very active and loving and is calling us to repentance.

8:13 *(The Interlude)*

A very brief interlude happens again. It is not long but it is a reminder. It comes from an eagle, whose high flight is well known.

It is from above, and like the series of seals, it warns that the worst is yet to come.

Points To Ponder

What happened when the seventh seal was opened?

Upon whom were these judgments brought?

What were some of the signs? Are there any signs today?

Chapter 9

9:1-11 ***(The Fifth Trumpet)***

With the blowing of this trumpet we are introduced to the bottomless pit. Since it is a pit, it signifies "down." Whenever we refer to heaven we somehow signify an "up" direction. There is no doubt that in those days most people pictured a three-story universe. How much they saw this to be geographical is debatable, but theologically both the Old and New Testaments leave little doubt that up signifies "with God" and down means "separation from God."

Things are so bad this time that people will actually seek death (9:6). The happenings of the first four trumpets had an indirect effect upon people, but this trumpet releases a direct result upon mankind. Yet those who have the seal will not be harmed (9:4). Again in the midst of fear is the reassurance.

The pit has as its king an angel. Angels were viewed as messengers of God. They were considered doers of good. Some have seen fit to believe this fallen angel is the devil who makes people do wrong things. This is neither biblical nor good theology. John's writings show that human sin is the cause of evil in the world. To see anything other than this is to remove the responsibility of humankind. With removal of the option of being responsible or irresponsible we become mere puppets to be manipulated by a good God and a bad devil. Furthermore, if we have been symbolic this far in our many understandings of this writing, there is no reason to quit now. The fallen angel dramatically personifies the evil that people bring upon themselves through their sin. And it is our own responsibility which separates us from God, rather than an outside power which gives us no choice.

The plague of locusts was a most feared event in John's day. Some areas of the United States have felt the effects of these plagues at various times in history. Trees are stripped, crops are ruined, and they can be so thick as to fill the sky like smoke.

Adding to this picture is that these locusts won't do the normal type of destruction, but rather attack people directly with the sting of a scorpion. Scorpions are poisonous but only a few are deadly. Their sting is a very painful and irritating wound.

Once again this should strike fear and repentance into the heart of the unbeliever. These locusts are even dressed up with hair, teeth, scales, and tails. It is pictures like these which make Revelation so difficult for most people to understand. We tend to get literal, and the picture becomes so unreal that we just scratch our heads and push it aside. Apocalypses are dramatic, symbolic, and stretch truths to their ultimate extremes to make their point.

This section must be viewed with the historic enlightenment of what fear locusts struck in the minds and lives of people. They were Destroyers, which is what *Abaddon* and *Apollyon* mean. The key to understanding the whole sequence of episodes comes in 9:20ff when we hear about the people's lack of repentance.

9:12-21 ***(The Sixth Trumpet)***

Think of the fear that this picture brings. Invasion from the East by a cavalry of 200,000 would certainly be a warning to the people.

Why must woe be piled upon woe? Hasn't there been enough? Again we point out that these are not necessarily to be seen as progressing one after another. If we saw them that way, the fractions effected (one-thirds and one-fourths) would eventually add up to the whole number one, and the end would have arrived before it actually happened.

With this warning we find another direct attack. But remember, John even gives us a reminder in verse 17 that this is still a vision. We need not go into great detail on the picture, as much would be repetitious.

But why so many woes, why so many attacks? Verses 20 and 21 show us the reason: God's hope for repentance. Even though they didn't repent, God doesn't stop trying. These two verses are the keys to our entire understanding. The purpose is repentance. But even with the warnings people continue on in their own way. They did not stop their crimes of murder, cheating, immorality, or thievery, but worse yet, they continued their worship of idols and of the works of their own hands.

Is this really any different from today? Caught up in a material world, we worship all the goods we can accumulate. People spend more money on recreation than they give to the church. The cosmetic industry is a multi-billion dollar business. Advertising is directed at youthfulness, sexuality, and earthly success. The work of our hands becomes more important than the work of God's hands. We receive scores of warnings ranging from inflation, rising crime rates, and political scandals to pollution, natural imbalance, and drugs. Yet humankind continues to worship their gods and idols rather than the God of love who cares for us and calls us to repentance.

As you read this always remember the large truths. Don't get caught and bewildered on the small descriptions.

Points To Ponder

Who is spared from harm in these destructions? (hint: v. 4)

Of what sins are the people guilty? Are we guilty of these today?

Who hopes what will happen as a result of these attacks?

How many people are affected by the attacks?

Chapter 10

This is a rather long section. The interlude has three parts. The first part includes the introduction and then a sealing of another series of seven before it is opened. The second part is called the bitter scroll. The third deals with two witnesses having the power to prophesy. We also have the seventh trumpet, which is a most reassuring section, as it announces the impending end. As you work through this section make sure you take ample time to read and reread 11:15-19.

10:1-7 ***(The Mighty Angel and the Seven Thunders)***

The entire interlude of which these verses are a part is a very dramatic section. After the six pronouncements of the first six trumpets we are really ready for the final blast. The interlude is very important. It affords us a pause in the midst of all these judgments to step back and assess the opportunities which God does gives us for repentance.

In this case we not only have a pause in the series of seven, but another whole series flashes before us. The signal that it is a series is given by the seer who said he was about to write (v. 4). But a voice says, "Hold it, wait a minute, seal it up and do not write," for "there should be no more delay" (v. 6).

What were these seven thunders? Very simply, we don't know. Anyone who speculates about their meaning is only guessing and trying to make this message fit a theory where all words have to fit into their exact place.

Now the mighty angel offers us a different picture. This one we know something about from previous sections of the book. The angel is wrapped in a cloud and has a face like the sun and legs like pillars of fire. All of these things, sun, clouds, and fire, are part of creation. This creation was of God. He was in charge of it and he still is. This is further emphasized by his right foot on the sea and his left foot on the land. All of God's creation comes into play in the Book of Revelation. It is only right, if this world is to end and judgment come upon it, that all of creation be included both in the judging and in the being judged. One thing was omitted above. That was the rainbow. In the midst of judgment is the promise. The rainbow and its pot of gold is thought of more in terms of a fairy tale today, but the rainbow is a biblical sign of the promise. The rainbow is a promise of the sun shining in the midst of rain. This goes back to the story of Noah (Genesis 9:8-17).

While we couldn't say more about the thunders above, it does serve a purpose in helping us learn more about the seer.

No one knows exactly how the whole vision we call the Revelation took place or how John recorded it. We do not know how long this vision took; was it minutes, hours, days? However long it took place, it is doubtful that John was writing simultaneously to his seeing the vision. It just could be that under divine inspiration he is reflecting on the thunders and is about to write when he thinks, "Oh, come on, John, let's not get bogged down in details, let's get on with it."

The message of this vision which is repeated numerous times is that those who have turned against God will not repent and must face judgment. Even with the continual assurance which is carried to the believers, this is anything but a happy role in which the seer finds himself. Anyone who is loved by God and knows it, loves others in response. Christians should be deeply concerned for unbelievers. We cannot sit back and laugh, saying, "I told you God would get you." We can only sorrow over the loss because we love them.

10:8-11 *(The Little Scroll)*

It is very difficult to know where to start our explanation of these four verses. So let's keep our train of thought from above going which dealt with Christian love. This will help us understand the bitterness of the scroll. Our first reaction to the love of God in Christ is the sweetness of grace. It brings freedom, it brings joy. But a different aftertaste comes when we realize this sweetness is for all people and many turn their backs to it. Because we love them and care for them, it is bitter news to us that they should be lost. One warning must be made to today's Christians. We walk a fine line between the knowledge of God's judgment upon mankind and doing the judging ourselves. Our job, like John's (v. 11), is to tell the good news, and that good news infers a message to the unrepentant.

Now let's go back to the angel who is introduced in verse 1 and is given a little scroll (v. 9). The seer once again becomes part of the action as he is instructed to take it and eat it. This episode can show us the importance of understanding this message symbolically. Literally it looks like some "nut" eating parchment. If he was dumb enough to eat it, it should have made him sick.

But if we see this symbolically, that is, to look for the message represented by this scene, it almost explodes with meaning.

Ezekiel 2:8—3:3 has a similar episode. In Ezekiel, as here, it is a message of God's love which calls for repentance. The only difference between the two is that it does not become bitter to Ezekiel. For John, the times have changed. He has experienced, like Ezekiel, how hard-hearted the people of God are to a message of repentance.

If we relate this little scroll to the gospel of Jesus Christ, we can get the full impact. First of all, John, like Ezekiel, eats the scroll. This is symbolic of digesting the message thoroughly. At first the message is sweet. The seer reads about the grace of God loving us so much that he sent his Son to die for our sins. That is great, that is Good News, that is gospel. But his love calls for a response. We respond to God in faith and love, trusting not in ourselves but in him. The two verses back in 9:20-21 make it obvious that the people do not trust in God but rather in gods of their own making. Since the gospel message implies judgment upon the unrepentant (the repentant sinner is forgiven through the sacrifice of Christ), the scroll becomes bitter. John knows the people will not repent, and the message of the scroll which he must share is one of judgment and wrath. It's bitter, but it must be done.

Points To Ponder

How did the scroll taste at first? Then later?

Will those who have turned against God repent?

How do you think John was feeling by now about the vision he is sharing?

Chapter 11

11:1-14 *(The Two Witnesses)*

Turn to the Old Testament and read Zechariah 4:1-14 to get a flavor for this section. It also shows how people familiar with the prophets would be able to understand the language of John's vision.

The revelation to Saint John draws heavily upon the figures of the Old Testament. This is only natural, since the books of the Old Testament were not thrown aside when the people became Christian, but were seen as fulfilled in Christ. They knew this message; the figures were familiar to John's readers and may even have added credibility to his writing.

The measuring of something is a symbol used by Ezekiel, Jeremiah, and again in Revelation 21. Sometimes it is a check by God to see how the people "measure up," or it could be a preliminary to rebuilding. In this case it is used as a way of preparing to preserve something.

The 1,260 days in verse 3 is a familiar number in an unfamiliar form. This is the length of time God's witnesses will prophesy, but it is also the same length of time that the nations will trample on the holy city. Taking this symbol from days to months and then one step further gives us three and a half years. Since seven is such an important number in this book, one-half of that number should also mean something. If seven is complete, then one-half of seven would be incomplete. In this case, the period of time represented probably means a limited time as opposed to a complete or whole time like seven.

The witnesses are described as two olive trees and lampstands. The imagery is borrowed from the Old Testament, as the reading in Zechariah showed. The purpose of these witnesses is much the same as the happenings in nature, that is, to call attention to the unrepentant position of the people.

Verses 5 and 6 lead us to think that the witnesses remind the people of Moses and Elijah. The Old Testament concludes with these two in Malachi 4:4-6 and they are met again in the transfiguaration of our Lord (Matthew 17:1-13). These two witnesses are symbols that God does not leave his message without witnesses.

Even when they are killed, there is only a limited time of merrymaking, described as three and a half days (v. 9). This merrymaking takes place in the great city where the Lord was crucified. This is none other than Jerusalem. It is described allegorically as Sodom and Egypt. We remember the faithless people of Sodom from the Old Testament story of Abraham and Lot. They were wild, sin-filled, and self-worshiping. Egypt was enemy territory. So we have a picture of a city which opposed the message of God spiritually (like Sodom) and physically (like Egypt). It is only fitting to describe the place where our Lord was crucified in such a manner.

Dramatic things then happen. The witnesses are killed. The people rejoice that no one is around to keep harping at them and their foolish ways. It doesn't end there, because these two witnesses share in a resurrection (11:11-13) which includes an earthquake, further stressing that God is in control.

The scene is very reminiscent of the crucifixion scene where lots were cast for Jesus' garments, people jeered, and soldiers mocked him. But those who share the message of Christ also share the resurrection and ascension (11:11-12). This was a marvelous assurance to those who faced possible martyrdom in John's day.

Historically speaking, this scene has repeated itself. When the true witnesses are gone and the unbelievers mock the church, God acts dramatically. One can readily think of such great witnesses as Augustine, Luther, Calvin, Bohhoeffer, and Pope John XXIII who saw sleeping churches and brought renewed life to them.

11:15-19 *(The Seventh Trumpet)*

Are these words familiar? Anyone who has ever heard Handel's *Messiah* recognizes verse 15. This great triumph song is a strong example of the use of the proleptic feeling. The scene to come, the promise for the believer, is so full of help and assurance that in the seer's eye or ear it is present already.

Flashing back on the screen come the 24 elders of chapters 4 and 5. They sing a song of thanksgiving which stresses the reign of God and the time for judgment. This is not scary; it is the hope, the goal, the destination, and expectation of all believers.

This triumph song is the turning point in the Book of Revelation. It speaks of what went before (the rage of the nations) and what lies ahead (the rewarding of servants and destroying the destroyers).

The great assurance of this message is in the viewing of the open temple and the ark of the covenant being seen. The covenant between God and his people is a basic part of the story of the Old Testament. It was made at Mount Sinai but was prefigured with Noah (Genesis 6:18) and with Abraham and his descendants (Genesis 22:15-18). The ark was the symbol of God's presence from Sinai into the promised land. When the prophecies of the coming Christ are told by the prophets, they speak of a new covenant (Jeremiah 31:31-34). Now at this turning point the assurance is that the covenant is still there between God and his people.

But is this really it? The end, I mean. Well, yes and no! That's the feeling of the proleptic. We know more is coming with the signs of lightning, thunder, earthquake, and hail. Will this be the final judgment?

Points To Ponder

What is the purpose of measuring the temple?

What is the significance of the witnesses?

What is the message of the triumph song? Can we hear it today?

Chapter 12

Introduction

This section extends from chapter 12 through chapter 14. With these three chapters we begin one of the ways to view the final judgment. It is the triumph song of the preceding chapters through which the transition is made from partial judgment to complete judgment. Complete judgment is, by nature of its completeness, final. The final judgment is depicted in the Book of Revelation in three ways. This three-chapter section is the first. It is an unnumbered series which dramatically portrays the life on this earth and its end as a great conflict between two powers. Following this will be a numbered series of seven bowls. Following that series there is another detailed description of the final judgment.

Some scholars have felt that this section, Revelation 12:1—14:20, is also a series of seven events with an interlude between the sixth and seventh happenings. How important this is can be debated. If one has a theory that the total book revolves around the number seven, then this must be a series of seven. If, on the other hand, you only consider seven to be a very important number in the understanding of this book, it isn't necessary to prove that the seer consciously made this an unnumbered series of seven. This author agrees that there are seven happenings or episodes in these chapters, but the message is more important than the form. Seven is important but not of such great importance that we forget the message.

We have stressed the dramatic approach which an apocalyptic writer uses. When anyone writes about great conflict which affects the final destiny of people, it must be dramatic. It is a life-and-death situation. But this struggle brings out another emphasis or characteristic of this type of writing. Apocalyptic literature is dualistic. It is the recording of the struggle of the perfect God who cares for his creation which has chosen of its own free will to be imperfect. The inner struggle within each person between that which he does and that which he knows he should do can also become collective when society chooses to do what it wants and finds itself opposed to the will of God.

These three chapters (12-14) afford us the opportunity to deal with one of the sticky issues of theology: the devil. Overemphasis on the devil as a power at work outside of humankind draws away from the human's natural desire to sin and do wrong or serve self. This writer will downgrade the devil and emphasize our evil or selfish nature in order to bring balance back to the concept of evil. Our purpose is not to dispose or dismiss the devil but to retain the responsibility which humans have to their creator God. Without that, we are but pawns or animals.

12:1-17 *(The Conflict)*

The first happening in this struggle between the power of good and the power of evil is depicted as a sneaky dragon waiting to devour a mother and her child. One doesn't have to guess too hard about the identity of the mother and child. It is Jesus and his mother. Again a warning must be made about being too literal with this. This Halloween picture of the dragon conjures up all kinds of weird ideas about the power of evil upon the earth. Unless we remember that the power of evil is inherent within humankind, we are abdicating the responsibility of our lives in favor of being pawns in a chess game between God and the dragon.

If we jump ahead a few verses, Revelation 12:17 gives us the meaning in this. Christ was the victor over evil himself, but evil continues to permeate our lives, and we do battle with this evil daily, even as Christians.

This evil is personified in four ways in this chapter. Revelation 12:9 lists them all. Two are descriptive: serpent and dragon. Two are proper names: Devil and Satan. All of them are one and the same. All of them are ways of depicting evil.

When we consider that Jesus lived for more than thirty years, we begin to capture the feeling of this struggle. We remember his temptation in the wilderness (Matthew 4:1-11), his criticism from the Pharisees (Matthew 12:1-8, 15:1-20, and so forth), his chances to give the scribes and elders the answers they wanted in his trial (Matthew 26:57-68), or his chances miraculously to scare people into believing at the crucifixion (Matthew 27:40). All of these events in Christ's life show the presence of evil in the world during his life and ministry. This evil (the dragon) could not take control of (devour) him, and he died, arose, and ascended. The first episode shows God as victor.

It is interesting that evil is such a great power that it carries the struggle or conflict right into the place where God dwells. That takes some real gall. We might wonder how and when this took place or even where. Heaven is not description enough to satisfy most of us. But to ask these questions truly misses the point. The message is used to portray the extent to which evil goes in order to try to overcome the good and gracious God.

Since the dragon could not devour the child, the child rises to God. The dragon follows Christ to heaven and gets kicked out (12:9). What next? Since the big battle was lost, the devil goes back after the woman (mother of the child) in the wilderness.

This second happening is as dramatic as the first. The significance of the devil's getting tossed out of heaven in 12:9 is the assurance that heaven is safe from evil. An important aspect is that the blood of the Lamb is what conquers evil. We say that Jesus was sacrificed for our sins, and that is just what we mean. The blood of the Lamb conquers evil.

We must zero in on the message of verse 11 that the blood of the Lamb has overcome this evil and those who dwell with God will do so without this menacing presence of evil.

Another message is present in verse 12. Even though Christ overcame evil on our behalf, as long as we dwell on earth, evil will be present. Evil has been kicked out of heaven, but its presence and influence will always be felt on the earth.

And evil doesn't give up. Evil's presence on earth continues to struggle for superiority and chases the mother who gave birth to the child. Remember this mother had twelve stars for a crown, symbolizing God's elect for the church. This is very dramatic, for we know that Mary, mother of Christ, was not a leader in the church, although she may have been active in the movement to follow Christ. Literalists have to pass over such sections as this or twist them to fit their formulas. But if we view this as a dramatic symbolism of an important truth, we gain understanding.

That important truth is that evil is very much present in the world, just as the church is in the world, and evil seeks to infiltrate the company of believers.

Points To Ponder

Knowing the history of Jesus, how did the dragon try to devour him?

What happens to the dragon? Of what is this symbolic?

Where does the dragon go? Is it still there today?

Chapter 13

Inroduction

The dragon cannot do the job himself, so he commissions two beasts to try to do his work for him. His work or goal is the turning of people away from God. One beast rises out of the sea (13:2), and one comes from the earth (13:11). The earthly beast does work that serves the interest of the sea beast.

When we know where to look for evil we can put up some sort of a defense against it. Our awareness alone is some defense. But when evil comes disguised, it is more difficult to recognize. This episode is a case of disguise.

13:1-10 *(The Sea Beast)*

The fourth episode in this unnumbered group of happenings is a beast rising out of the sea. Who is this beast? The second part of 13:2 tells that whoever it is, the dragon has given it his power, throne, and authority. The sea is considered the symbol of human government. When countries were attacked in those days, the enemy often came by sea. It was easiest to travel, afforded the greatest surprise element, and also the quickest retreat if necessary. Thus the beast from the sea must symbolize human government.

As stated in the introduction, since the dragon could not accomplish his purpose by himself, he delegates authority. Since his purpose was to make war on the mother's offspring (12:17), we can be prepared for something evil in opposition to the church. This speculation quickly becomes fact as people begin to worship the dragon or the beast (13:4). That the attack is made upon believers is brought out in the call for the endurance of the saints (13:10).

Often we think of government as having its flaws, but not necessarily evil in the way it is seen here. In the United States we tend to think that as long as government leaves the church alone, it is all right. Few of us have ever been under authoritarian rule like our ancestors were or like John's friends were experiencing. The great problem outlined here was that this government has the people worshiping it. Government can be an institution of God as long as it doesn't make requirements which are in opposition to the purpose of God or belief in God.

13:11-18 *(The Earth Beast)*

Knowing the first beast is the government, together with a little Roman history, enables us to identify the second beast. The key is Revelation 13:12, a basic job description which shows the second beast making people worship the first beast.

Roman history records the widespread cults which engaged in emperor worship in the late first century. These cults had their own temples and priests. People came from distances to pay homage at these temples. It is even told that some of them had the emperor's image rigged with hinges and wires to make it move. Thus the second beast symbolizes pagan religion.

13:18 *(666)*

The second beast even has a number, 666. Throughout history many attempts have been made to identify this beast as one person in history. To reach that point, a language must be numerically coded with each letter representing a number. Then a formula has to be developed to reach a conclusion. Centuries ago, Protestants identified a number of popes in this manner and Roman Catholics retaliated by making the code come out to Martin Luther or John Calvin. Others have been able to formulate other names. It depends upon whom one wants to slander, and then one works out the formula.

More important to our study is that this number is composed of sixes. Six is one less than seven. Seven is the perfect or complete number. Six is a little less than seven, therefore this depicts someone a little less than perfect. Since humankind's fall into sin, isn't the human race a little less than perfect? Thus 666 simply depicts a human, who under the guise of religion serves the government.

Most scholars would agree that 666 referred to Nero as far as John's readers were concerned. Nero had died some 25 years before John received this revelation, but during his reign he had severely persecuted Christians. The tradition persisted that he would be reincarnated some day. When his name was written in Greek and coded, it deciphered to 666. When done in Latin it deciphers to 616. It is interesting to note that some early manuscripts of good authority use 616 instead of the 666 we find in our Bibles today.

This doesn't mean that it has no significance for us. When any government sets out to dominate people with its rule and force them to worship their leaders or those leaders' actions, it becomes an end in itself. As such, these men are strictly the work of their own hands and appropriately are given only a limited human number. They are no longer an institution of God but rather an institution opposed to God.

Points To Ponder

Who are the two beasts and what do they symbolize?

Who is 666? (Remember numbers have meanings.)

Chapter 14

14:1-5 *(The Lamb)*

This happening is the sixth unnumbered event, if you're keeping count. Our first five episodes were given over to a dramatic portrayal of evil at work in the world. Our sixth episode shows that God is not standing by, but is at work redeeming his people. Endurance is always needed in the face of evil. A picture of promise like this one produces that endurance.

Numerous figures which we have met before are involved with the Lamb in these verses. We meet the 144,000 again as well as the elders and the creatures from way back in the worship scene of chapters 4 and 5. These figures are spotless. Remember they were cleansed in the blood of the Lamb.

But what happened to the multitude from chapter 7? It is not an excuse to say we don't know. John is no doubt writing under a high degree of excitement and he could have forgotten to write it down or just inferred it. Some think that the grouping in 14:6, the next verse, takes care of it, but in chapter 7 this multitude was pictured as being before the throne and Lamb and not still bound to the earth. These are some questions we can't answer, but we must trust God who is constant in his love, which he reveals time and time again in this message.

14:6-13 *(The Interlude)*

Since the episodes are not numbered, we must do some guessing that this is an interlude. It is not very difficult to do, inasmuch as these three angels come between the two figures of Christ (14:1 and 14:14) at the climax or ending of the judgment. The interlude provides us with a message from the three angels. With the Lamb on Mount Zion (14:1-5) we were ready for the end, for the glorious scene of heaven, but this interlude is necessary to proclaim God's hour (the work of the first angel), announce Rome's fall (second angel), and show the fate of Rome's worshipers (third angel).

The angels' purpose is to proclaim an eternal gospel (14:6). One cannot help but wonder about all those people who are worshiping the beast, if the end is really coming. So here is the answer. They got what their earthly life brought upon them. The picture of wrath, anger, and torment fits their selfish life on earth.

The beautiful assurance of Revelation 14:13 is used in many funeral services. Think what it meant to the believers in John's day, or the imprisoned Christians under Nazi Germany in the 1940s, or any believer who has suffered for the faith.

14:14-20 *(The Reaper)*

Jesus Christ has been pictured as a Lamb in verses 1-5 and now as a reaper at the close of the same chapter. Verse 15 is the key that this depicts the final judgment. "The harvest of the earth is fully ripe." This is for the righteous. The unrighteous or unrepentant are pictured as grapes gathered and pressed by the wrath of God.

From this we see that all people are subject to God. Each chooses of his own free will how he responds to God. But God is ultimately the judge of our worth. None of us deserves the victory, but Christ has won the victory for those who trust in his sacrifice. In the end it is God who judges. The conflict is over, the battle is won for those who believe. With each of us there is an internal battle which goes on daily. In whom do we trust for our hope? Is it ourselves, or is it the Lamb?

Very dramatically we are seeing a picture of the doctrinal truth of Christ's second coming. We believe that in his first coming he came to save, and we profess his second coming will be to judge. This judgment is twofold, on the righteous and the unrighteous. It is dramatically pictured like a reaper putting his sickle to the harvest. That this is Christ is obvious by the use which John makes of the phrase "one like the son of man."

So the good are reaped and the bad are pressed down and trodden. Need we add more?

Points To Ponder

Jesus is pictured two ways in this chapter. What are they and why?

Who falls? Who really is Babylon?

What is reaped by the reaper? (Hint: there are two things reaped)

Chapter 15

Introduction

The previous episode of the beasts, the dragon, the lamb, the reaper, and so on, interpreted the final judgment as a struggle between the forces of good and the forces of evil. Chapters 15 and 16 also deal with the final judgment, but as a series somewhat similar to the seals and the trumpets. The similarity is found in the structure rather than the content, meaning there will be a listing of the first six items, then an interlude, and finally the seventh of the series.

Remember that these plagues do not have to be seen as a progression of events. The very fact that each of them is complete is what's important.

Various characters like a dragon, a beast, a lamb, and a reaper brought the first version of the final judgment. I stated that the Book of Revelation contains three versions of the final judgment. Here is a glance back and a glance ahead at how they line up.

Version 1	*Revelation 12:1—14:20*	*A Great Struggle*
Version 2	*Revelation 15:1—16:21*	*The Seven Bowls*
Version 3	*Revelation 17:1—18:24*	*A Detailed Account*

Our consideration in this chapter is part of the second version called "The Bowls." It is a numbered series with a little different look. There is a rather long preparation which is followed by the pouring of the first six bowls. When they are poured, it goes boom, boom, boom, one, two, three. There are no details outside of mentioning on whom the bowl is poured and its result.

This is probably the only way which the human mind can conceive of this judgment or the best way in which limited human words can be used to describe an act of God. The end of this world will probably not be accomplished in seven neat steps which progressively follow one another. The seven steps are listed to show completeness. The power of God is beyond the language and comprehension of earthly people. We need guides, illustrations, and listings to help our understanding. That is probably why there are three different ways that the final judgment is presented. Now let's look at the seven bowls.

15:1-8 *(The Preparation)*

Prior to the pouring of the bowls, there is an elaborate preparation. The bowls will be different from the seals and the trumpets in one great way. Their judgment will no longer be partial but will be complete.

Be careful to note that the plagues (verse 1) are not the series, but plagues are what will be contained in the bowls which the angels pour out. At first glance this looks almost like the seven thunders which jumped on the screen and then off. It isn't. This first verse is the introduction and preparation for the series, which could be called by the more descriptive title of "The Seven Bowls of Plagues."

The completeness of this pouring or judgment is emphasized with the words "for with them, the wrath of God is ended" (15:1).

Something fantastic is about to happen. The temple of the tent of witness is opened. We all can recall the Holy of Holies in the Jerusalem Temple which only the High Priest could enter, and then he did it only once a year. This sacred story was well known to John's people who had Jewish background, and this temple of the tent would symbolize something divine about to happen.

And here come our four living creatures getting into the act again, handing the bowls of God's wrath to the angels. We are now almost ready for the series of the final judgment, depicted as a pouring of wrath from bowls.

The Old Testament imagery in this section is obvious as the seer identifies the song of Moses. The poem which follows (vv. 3-4) is an abbreviated version of the ideas presented in the Song of Moses in Exodus 15. The sea of glass could be a reminder of the crossing of the Red Sea by the Israelites under the leadership of Moses. This crossing was an important event to the people of God. It showed God's presence in history, his guidance of his people, and his power over the enemy. It was through this sea that Moses led his people into the promised land.

But this song is also the song of the Lamb. It is associated with Moses' song, for the Lamb, the Christ of God, will lead us as we cross the sea from death to life, from mortality to immortality, from hope to fulfillment.

And now the bowls.

Points To Ponder

Why would the rejoicing be described as a Song of Moses and of the Lamb?

What is so important about opening the temple of the tent of witness?

Chapter 16

16:1-12 *(The First Six Bowls)*

The effects of the pouring will once again remind us of the plagues of Egypt (Exodus 7-11). Only this time, in contrast to Revelation 8:7ff, the fractions will be missing.

(Bowl 1) We recall the earth beast who symbolized pagan religion and see God's wrath in the form of sores directed upon those who followed the beast.

(Bowl 2) The symbol of the area of false government is next as the sea turns to blood.

(Bowl 3) The river and its contents, drinking water, are next; they too become blood.

(Bowl 4) The sun increases its heat and people curse God. Even with all this they still do not repent.

(Bowl 5) Even the throne of the beast must go. Nothing of this evildoer will remain. Again there is no repentance.

(Bowl 6) We are here reminded of the sixth trumpet which warned of the great cavalry approaching from the East.

The pouring of the bowls is quick. There is no use stalling around, as men are not going to repent. Most of the destruction is easily understood. All the elements of creation are treated: the seas, the rivers, the sun, and the beast's kingdom (earth). Humankind remains in this picture, but realistically speaking, how long can you live without water, heat, or land? That is why these can't be seen as progressive actions, but more probably instantaneous completeness. This holds true for the seventh bowl as well.

16:13-16 *(The Interlude)*

The evil one is still shown as trying to accomplish wrong in the midst of this end of the world. If the end is instantaneous, why have this? Or why show the battle taking shape?

We know from the history of humankind that the forces of evil are always at work in the world. We battle them individually within ourselves and collectively as the body of Christ on earth. This reality is ever with us, and it continues to the very end. The interlude shows us that evil has reached such an extreme that even in the midst of its own judgment it is still trying to do its thing.

The interlude is very closely tied to the first six bowls. Even in their destruction the three evil characters of chapters 12-14 emit spirits which try to bring evil to the world. The spirits are like frogs. This should have brought comfort to the believer. All the many fear-striking plagues on the unbelievers were real enemies of humankind, like the locusts or the earthquake. But frogs are just harmless croaking creatures of the pond.

Like other interludes, think about the element of assurance this brought to the believer. The great evil power, once a beast, becomes nothing more than a frog. The believer should remember to be ready and waiting for this moment. The thief in the night idea is stated by Christ in Matthew 24:43 and by Paul in 1 Thessalonians 5:2.

Armageddon has been a target or rallying point for some sect groups. Literalists who follow this book's chapters in periods of history must reach this point and forecast a battle between God's troops and the beast's troops. This is man's thinking. We think that God operates our way, and our way is to fight a war in order to conquer. The battle preparation is rather a symbolic way of showing that evil never gives up trying to conquer good until the end. This is indicative of the dualistic nature of apocalyptic literature.

16:17-21 *(The Seventh Bowl)*

The finality of this judgment is wrapped up with the destruction of the air. The earth, sun, and water are gone, and now the air. What's left? Nothing! The picture is completed with more happenings in nature which remind us of God's power and might.

God's ways are not man's ways and the seventh bowl shows that. God doesn't need an army to destroy evil and bring his first creation to a close. He simply destroys the air and pronounces, "It is done." When air is gone, all life is gone. Need more be said?

No, but wait, what about the people? They, too, are gone. This is judgment, and judgment is caused by the sin of people. God does not judge nature and institutions, He judges people. But where did the people go? What happened? This is so obvious from the message of the Gospel and the preceding chapters that it is taken for granted here. The details of the closing chapters 19-21 will clarify this further.

Points To Ponder

This reminds us of the plagues of chapter 8, but what's different this time?

What does the beast become and how does this assure us?

What battles between good and evil are going on in today's world?

Chapter 17

Introduction

If we were limited to stating only one overall theme for the Book of Revelation, it would be judgment. We have learned that there are other important items in this book, such as assurance to believers, conflict between good and evil, encouragement to the churches, and finally a promise of the new earth. Yet the majority of this work deals with God's judgment.

From chapters 6-11 we studied and read about judgments which were limited in their effect, but still very devastating. With chapter 12 we began to read about the final judgment in terms of a dramatic struggle between good and evil. In chapters 15 and 16 the pouring of the bowls depicted the final judgment as a numbered series. Now beginning with chapter 17 and continuing through chapter 20 we will trace the final judgment in more detail. This section, like chapters 12-14, is an unnumbered series of events. Some writers see seven events pictured in chapters 17-20. Whether or not there are seven makes little difference. By the time we reach this point in the message, the importance of seven is fully understood. We are reaching the climax of all things, and many things start happening all at once. The condemnations are strong, the assurances are powerful, and the songs are mighty. This is it — the last written portrayal of the final judgment.

Now as you read, picture yourself as a member of a very small group of people living in a nation where the vast majority of people and its leaders are greedy and self-serving, treating people like animals, and not too happy about your little group getting together regularly to worship some god they don't even recognize. How do you feel as this picture becomes real?

17:1-6 *(The Harlot)*

Babylon, an Old Testament community and empire, was continually a threat to the children of Israel, the people of the promise. It was a rich and at times powerful nation, but the use of the name in the Old Testament was always found in connection with a threatening pagan power.

The Roman Empire, with its central city of Rome, was the pagan power which threatened the early Christian church of John's day. The Christians now considered themselves the people of the promise. So Rome was to the early Christians what Babylon was to the Israelites.

When we presume that this message somehow passed through official Roman hands on its way to the churches (since John was in prison), we easily understand why John did not write "Fallen, fallen is Rome the Great." It would have never made it. So Babylon is without a doubt John's word for Rome and its empire. This was previously alluded to in Revelation 14:8.

All of this leads us to greater understanding of the coming chapters where the name Babylon repeatedly pops up.

The harlot of this vision is "seated upon many waters" (Revelation 17:1). Babylon was located at the convergence of the waters which emptied into the present Persian Gulf. These waters included the great Tigris and Euphrates Rivers. These waters were used for trade, just like the water which made Rome an important port.

Rome is described symbolically as a harlot because the Roman government gave other nations temporary pleasure in exchange for her own getting rich. She is described as committing fornication with kings to show symbolically that many of the agreements between the Roman Empire and other nations were mutually agreeable but ethically questionable. If we look closely at history, we learn of the shady dealings of some of the emperors. These dealings made the citizens stand in awe of the government and worship her. The writing describes this as citizens (or dwellers or inhabitants) becoming drunk.

The seer is invited to come and view the judgment of the harlot. We have seen this type of involvement before. And now he is carried away to view it. The location of the wilderness is probably a reference to his getting an objective view of things. The wilderness would be a quiet place where there would be no obstruction to his understanding. Didn't Jesus go to the wilderness where he was tempted? And the temptation gave him an objective view of the ministry of overcoming evil which lay before him.

The woman (harlot, whore) to be judged is seated on a beast. She is robed in scarlet and purple, full of abominations, and drunk. This picture is in direct contrast to the bride which will be pictured in Revelation 19:7-8 who is clothed in fine linen which symbolizes righteous deeds. We will see this further in Revelation 21:2, where the New Jerusalem is a bride adorned.

17:7-18 *(The Personification of the Harlot)*

As stated above the harlot depicts the evil doings of the Roman Empire. The harlot is figurative, so who actually does all these evil things? Our vision shows a beast with seven heads and ten horns. It carries the harlot (Revelation 17:7). In other words, whoever this beast is, it is the one who gets the job done for the harlot.

Verse 9 tells us the seven heads are seven hills, obviously referring to Rome which was famous for its seven hills. But they are also seven kings. John is offered an interpretation of the harlot and the beast. The beast is the vehicle by which the harlot gets around (Revelation 17:3). If the harlot depicts the evil doings of the empire, then the vehicle by which they are accomplished is the emperor.

It is these very verses in fact which serve as the best evidence available for locating the date of this writing. Here we get into a history of the Roman Emperors. Revelation 17:10 describes these seven kings (emperors). "Five of whom have fallen, one is ..." certainly has bearing upon the date. John seems to be living during the reign of what he considers the sixth emperor. There are many problems in tracing this and so we will list the emperors by name and date from the beginning of the empire.

1. Augustus	27 B.C.-A.D. 14
2. Tiberius	A.D. 14-37
3. Caligula	A.D. 37-41
4. Claudius	A.D. 41-54

5.	Nero	A.D. 54-68
	Galba Otho Vitellius	A.D. 68-69
6.	Vespasian	A.D. 69-79
7.	Titus	A.D. 79-81
8.	Domitian	A.D. 81-96

First of all we have omitted Galba, Otho, and Vitellius from the numbering. The reign of each was only for a few months, and none was in power long enough to gain the support of the people.

Now we can take the remaining eight and look at Revelation 17:8 and 10. Verse 10 is of greatest importance because of its clarity. Five kings or emperors have fallen, one is, the other has yet to come. On the basis of this alone, "the one who is" would be Vespasian, the sixth emperor. However, history records Vespasian as being one of the more business-like emperors, and there is no evidence of any religious persecution or imprisoning religious leaders like John during his reign.

Revelation 17:11 might be the key when it says "it is an eighth but it belongs to the seven." This sounds more like a math problem than history. There was a legend at Nero's death that he would return. Many felt that Domitian was Nero reincarnate. Certainly their styles of ruling were similar. Both were hard and authoritative. Both sought to rule out other religions and make the state cult the only worship form. With this understanding the date of writing could be placed at the time of Domitian. This also shows how highly the citizens regarded their emperors and to what extent their worship of them had gone.

There is indeed a problem with dating this work and one can understand why scholars argue about the date. The point of reference could be either during the reign of Nero or Domitian. That does not change the message. The message is obvious. Rome is like a harlot, and its forces of evil make things rough on the followers of the lamb.

At first, Revelation 17:15-18 is difficult to figure out. It looks like the people whom the harlot had doing her work turn against her. And that is just what the case is. Like people bringing judgment upon themselves, the empire engages in shady deals for her own benefit and ends up having the makers of those deals turn against her. The harlot's end is the result of her own greed.

Don't overlook verse 14. It is reminiscent of the struggles of chapters 12-14. The dualistic conflict between good and evil is ever-present in apocalyptic literature and reappears time and again in the Book of Revelation.

Points To Ponder

Of what sins is Babylon accused? How did this affect the Christian church?

The Lamb conquers the beast. Why? What is he?

Chapter 18

18:1-24 ***(Details of the Shady Deals)***

With chapter 17 so filled with symbolic history we must be careful that we don't miss the message. That message becomes clearer as we look at the harlot's fall in this chapter. Here we see all the details of the downfall of Babylon the harlot (Rome). The general description of verses 1-3 paints a picture of evil, greed, and conquest. They show just how foul this empire had become. This song of doom will echo throughout this chapter as we detail her evil deeds.

Her efforts have touched many nations. Empirical dealings for wanted luxuries were numerous, and many became rich because of them. The taxes of the people made all of this possible. The followers of God are encouraged to separate themselves from the situation.

We get an idea of just how far she has gone in her greed when we look at those who become part of the announcing of her doom. The announcers are both earthly and heavenly, for there is little in life which remains untouched by Rome's dealing and acts.

18:1	An angel calls out mightily
18:4	Another voice says
18:9	Kings weep and wail
18:11, 19	Merchants weep and mourn
18:17	Shipmasters and sailors cry out
18:21	Another angel speaks

The merchandise in which the business dealt is like a list of all the finery and luxury of the world (Revelation 18:11-13). This business even included people. The seer calls them slaves, and then clarifies by saying human lives (or souls). The affirmation which Jesus Christ made in his earthly life was that all are equal (see Matthew 25:31-46). He respected each individual for what he or she was. Slaves are people, and John shows that in his words.

The wailing, weeping, and mourning continue from all who dealt with the empire.

We must emphasize once more that this vision is of a divine act which can only be described in a limited way by the human mind and language. If we become too literal in our interpretation, it seems like only Rome is being judged. The others look like they are standing around watching what's going on. It is almost like sightseers at a fire. You watch, you feel bad, then you go home and forget about it.

Remember two things: 1) Rome was the world in those days. Yes, there were other nations, but none with the power and might of Rome. For all intents and purposes, Rome was the world for Christians. 2) Judgment is upon all people. Some of it will be good and some bad. It is dependent upon your either being washed in the blood of the Lamb or being caught up in the deeds of the harlot.

If the judgment is to come instantly, as stated previously, people won't be standing around watching. It will happen, boom! That's it! Then why show it this way? How else can it be shown in human language and understood by the human mind? If we only said, "Believers don't worry; you are saved and Rome is doomed," it would not have the emotional effect needed to encourage believers in their situations, nor would it be dramatic enough to make its point.

Furthermore, this descriptive elongation of the judgment process allows the scripture to become applicable to all ages as we see the similarity of nations and people serving themselves and as we feel the constant love of God with its promises ever present in our lives.

In reality her end does not take long. "In one hour" it all takes place (Revelation 18:9, 17). In fact, her end will come like a millstone thrown into the sea. We all know it doesn't exactly float. With the throwing of the millstone, verses 21-24 take us on a tour of a ghost town. All the celebrating, all the craftsmen, all the marrying are gone. The cause of her downfall was herself.

Even today, any nation which sets out to make itself wealthy at the expense of others and lets nothing get in its way will fall. A nation's own greed makes it blind to people's real needs and will eventually suffocate it in luxury and blindness. The message is clear. All things come from God, and to him must thanks be given. Life is bought by the blood of Christ, and concern and love must be our response to others.

Points To Ponder

Why do so many people of the world weep and wail when "Babylon" falls?

How is the final fall described?

Do you think the end of the world will come quickly or slowly? Why?

Chapter 19

Introduction

Chapter 19 contains what many scholars consider to be the third through sixth events in the series of seven that are contained in this last version of the final judgment. As this third version of the final judgment continues, you will note similarities and additions to the two other versions. The first version was a dramatic struggle, the second was a pouring of the bowls of wrath, and this third one is the most elaborate of the three. Why do we need three renditions of the final judgment if final means once and for all? I know of no other way to explain it than to say that if you don't understand it the first way, maybe the second will hit home to you, and if you don't understand the first or second description, maybe the third will get through to you.

This is it! There is no holding back now. The final judgment is under way. Chapters 17 and 18 covered the first two events in this vision of judgment. We saw the harlot and her deeds and then we saw the judgment of the harlot. The final judgment moves to completion as we view four more events or scenes from the final judgment in this chapter.

19:1-5 *(The Hallelujah Chorus)*

The harlot has been judged. Babylon has fallen. That greedy, deceitful, self-serving empire which made it tough to be a Christian is gone. The believers are free from occasional persecution, subtle harassment, and mental anguish. Free! Free! The heavens shout hallelujah.

Note how the elders and living creatures are present once more. When they first appeared in chapters 4 and 5, we said they would reappear often. Each time they are present they remind us that God is in charge and is doing the judging. This is evidenced by the fact that they are always around the throne.

Who gets the credit? God gets the credit. His judgments are true. He has avenged those who died witnessing for him. God is in charge. We always thought he was or at least we hoped he was. Now we know he was.

19:6-10 *(A Wedding Invitation)*

The happy chorus continues its hallelujahs. The proleptic anticipation of the Kingdom in Revelation 11:15-19 now becomes actual as the multitude proclaims that God reigns and to God belongs the glory.

"The marriage of the Lamb has come" (Revelation 19:7). The invitation is here. The bride is ready so we know this is not an engagement party. It is just before the wedding. From the Bible we know the church as the bride and Christ as the bridegroom (Matthew 9:14-15; Matthew 25:1-13; John 3:28-30). The bride's clothing is bright and pure. This compares to the gaudy purple, scarlet, and gold of the harlot. In addition we can note that it was granted the bride to dress this way. The linen is righteous deeds, but it was still *granted* her to dress this way. We walk the fine line of grace and works. Maybe we could say that grace puts us on the right path, and deeds help to keep us walking it.

Does the idea of righteous deeds bother us or make us fidget? Protestants have emphasized salvation by grace through faith so much that we often forget about deeds. Our concept of deeds is still locked into the five-hundred-year-old idea of buying relics and bones and gaining points for heaven. We don't want any part of that, but we'd better remember that good works are still important. The change brought in by the Reformation was not an abolition of good works. It was rather a change from buying your way into eternal life with God to the biblical stress on responding to God's grace and love.

Next, John learns that there is only one whom we can worship (Revelation 19:9, 10). He starts to bow to the angel and is startled to his senses with "You must not do that! ... Worship God!" Only God makes our marriage possible. Only God has the strength to destroy Babylon. Only to God is worship directed.

19:11-16 *(The Faithful and True)*

The fifth event is our third Christophany (picture of Christ). It flashes before us on a white horse, the steed of triumph. We learned in chapter 6 that triumph could be triumph of bad, but here it is obviously good. The rider is called the Word of God, King of Kings, Lord of Lords.

His weapon is a sharp sword. The uniqueness of this sword is that it issues from his mouth. He is called "The Word of God," so words are his weapon. A sword can be cutting and decisive. Jesus' words were that type of weapon. There are few neutral observers in the Gospels. They either become followers of Jesus or seek to stop him.

19:17-21 *(A Destruction Scene)*

From the beautiful picture of the upcoming wedding, the Faithful and True provided transition to this horrible scene. The beast and the false prophet are the same ones we met in the dramatic scenes of chapter 13. The false prophet is a little easier description for us to understand than the earth beast, but they are the same. These beasts were the guiding power of that harlot over whose fall heaven rejoices. It is only right that the beasts should also be destroyed. They are thrown into the lake of fire (Revelation 19:20). Fire is an evil thing. It destroys. It is uncontrollable. It was feared in John's day. A lake of fire would be a gruesome sight. It is the opposite of the peace and calm of the heavenly scenes. It is separation from God.

The remainder of the section is a dramatic description of the overthrow of the beasts.

Points To Ponder

Who is worshiping God? Where did we see them before?

Who are we admonished to worship by the angel?

The beast and the false prophet were thrown into the lake of fire. How were the rest of the evil ones "done away with"?

From where did the sword emanate?

Chapter 20

Introduction

We now arrive at the interlude and seventh event or scene in this final judgment. The form is the same. Six events, an interlude, and then the final event. Take your time. This is it. Read carefully and ask for the Spirit's guidance.

20:1-10 *(The Interlude)*

First the harlot, then the beasts who did the work of the harlot, and now the power which guided the beasts. This section portrays how that evil one, the dragon, the serpent, the devil, or Satan, whatever you call him, is dealt with. The first verses make it look like this is finally it, but then the interlude appears. Even in these final moments of the earth this evil power is sealed, but must be let loose after a while. Remember that the interlude's purpose is to provide assurance for the believers. Certainly tying up the devil for a thousand years is assuring. Like the beast and the prophet in the previous verses, this reminds us of the dragon in chapter 12. The dragon is thrown into the pit. Isn't that the place from which it came (Revelation 11:7)?

During this period of imprisonment of evil, we see a reassuring scene of the martyrs reigning with Christ. The time of this reign is called a thousand years (millennium). This is a very controversial item. Whole denominations have been formed on the basis of their interpretation of these thousand years. If all numbers in the book thus far have been symbolic, why not this one? In fact, it is very biblical to be symbolic with this number. One needs only to see the witness of the Psalmist (Psalm 90:4) and the words of 2 Peter 3:8 to begin to understand that time is something needed only by humankind. We speak of *days* of creation when the elements which govern it (sun and moon) weren't even created until the fourth day. Since God exists from eternity, he isn't too caught up in time.

To get literal with the thousand-year period means to look for that time in history when the thousand-year lockup of the Devil has begun or will begin. This would once again put the timing of judgment in human hands, which is opposed to the "thief in the night" concept of Jesus' own teaching.

We can really only speculate on the meaning of all this. If we get worried and spend our study on this mystery of the millennium, we will miss the main points of the book. We stated in our introduction that there were sections which contained mysteries and questions we couldn't answer. God is God and people are people. We can't fully understand God's power or his ways. We *can* know that power and trust in it through experience and promise. Whatever this vision depicts, we do know it is very reassuring.

There are also words of assurance to the believer who wonders about the martyrs. Even when evil forces are loosed once more, it isn't long before they are *finally* taken care of.

The nations of God and Magog are borrowed from Ezekiel 38:2. They represent the worst opponents of God's people. At his losing, Satan picks up where he left off, trying to subdue the good as lived by the people of God. But in the end God is still all-powerful and separates Satan from himself eternally by throwing him down to keep company with the beasts. And when Satan is cast down this time, it's "forever and ever" (Revelation 20:10).

20:11-15 *(The Throne Scene)*

The final event or scene is a picture of the throne. It is only proper that the last version of our judgment ends at the place where it began. The throne scene of chapters 4 and 5 introduced our series of partial and final judgments. The participants of that scene reappeared numerous times, and now we end the judgment where it began. Our focus is placed upon books. Again we see an attempt to put a divine event into human concepts. Will Saint Peter meet us at the gate to see if our name is listed? It is doubtful! But books are the places in which history is stated and records are kept. If God is all-knowing, he doesn't need books, but humankind needs books to remind us that God is all-knowing.

It is interesting to note that the lake of fire continues. It is not destroyed. The Bible teaches eternal life for everyone. But this life is either a life with God or separated from God. The lake of fire depicts the place of separation from God.

Points To Ponder

What is the purpose of this interlude of time?

What happens to the devil?

How are the dead judged by God? How will we be judged?

Chapter 21

Introduction

The judgment is behind us and we now look at the eternal future which follows the judgment. The final judgment is an everlasting earthly message intended for all people. In spite of all the symbolic applications to the Roman Empire, it is intended for all times in history. If we remember that, we are better prepared to deal with these concluding chapters. They were directed as a promise to the people of John's day, and they are also intended as a promise for us today.

With the judgments complete, we move quickly to the eternal home for all who believe. Many people within the church have a philosophic understanding of eternal life which is in conflict with the biblical understanding. They see separation of body and soul with souls floating around somewhere in the heavens with a spiritual God. That's philosophy and not biblical theology. The resurrection is an act of God which includes a new style of living. It is a life of harmony and beauty. It is a dynamic and active existence. God is present. The new heaven and the new earth are one. The when, where, and how of this we leave up to God. As chapter 21 unfolds we shall view this promise.

21:1-4 *(The New Heaven and the New Earth)*

John's remarks in verse 1 sum up in a very precise manner the Christian belief in eternal life. This was not a radical change in thought, since it was recorded earlier by the prophet in Isaiah 65:17 and 66:22. We can paraphrase this verse by saying the original creation of the world is destroyed, a new creation is established, and God will not be separated from his people. Heaven and earth are one.

This new earth, as beautiful as a bride on her wedding day, is called a New Jerusalem. It is compared to a city, which keeps the contrast with Babylon active. There is a gigantic difference between a bride and a harlot. One is new, fresh, vigorous, pure, lovely, and radiant. The other is used, tired-looking, covered with make-up, sneaky, and artificial.

If we knew nothing more about the promise than these four verses, they would be ample. The brief words of Revelation 21:3, which states "the dwelling of God is with men" or "the home of God is among mortals," are assurance beyond comprehension. This blends with the removal of the "sea of glass" in verse 1. We pointed out the potential theater setting in chapter 4 which showed the audience removed from the action by a sea of glass. This barrier has now been removed.

It is also possible that this sea refers to the seat of government. The beast from the sea represented governmental power. In either case, the message is the same. There are no more reasons to fear, God is with you.

The promise which stands out is that God himself will be with his people. It is a merging of heaven and the new earth. If we believe that God is a God of love and peace, we need not worry about where this will be or what it will be like. The presence of God is adequate promise to provide all the joyful anticipation we need. The remembrances of all sad earthly things are gone. There are no tears, no death, no mourning, no crying, and no pain.

21:5-8 *(Saved or Separated)*

We begin this section with a reminder that this is something new. There are two words in the Greek language (the original written language of the Book of Revelation) for "new." One describes something young and inexperienced. It corresponds closely to the English word "novice." The other word means new in the sense of unused or fresh. This latter word is the one John uses at this point.

God proceeds to call himself the Alpha and the Omega. This symbol is still retained by the church today. It describes not only his eternal nature, but his power to create and destroy. For the believer there is the added impact that God is not only our source of life, he is also our goal. We receive life from God, and our desire is to be with God. He is the Alpha and Omega. He makes this possible.

Through his conquering, he makes us conquerors. As a result we become his children. We enter into a family relationship with him. This is a comforting assurance to the reader. One needs only to remember the fears or anxieties which accompanied our leaving our parental homes to strike out on our own. Yes, there was the excitement of the freedom, but there was also the realization that now we no longer had ready access to parental support and guidance. God promises us that ready access in our eternal life on the new earth.

We can conjure up all kinds of ideas and speculations about when, where, and how all of this will happen, but nothing says it like God's own word: "It is done." That's all. It's done!

From here he makes all things new. There is a separation between the one who believes he has been cleansed by the blood of the conquering Lamb and those who haven't chosen to be so cleansed.

Those who have not looked at him as evidenced by their earthly deeds cast their lot with their leaders. This is the second death. In contrast to the access which the believer has with God, the unbeliever is separated. The first death is our earthly bodily death. The second death must refer to something different, since you do not die when you are already dead. Chapter 20:11-15 gave us some insight into this where it was revealed that all would be judged. This is evidenced by the fact that Death and Hades gave up their dead. (Hades referred to the place of the dead.) Thus all were judged.

The second death is the lake of fire. Without speculating on the where or what of this lake, we can simply contrast this to the statement that the believer will be with God. Thus the second death refers to the unbeliever being separated from God.

21:9-21 *(The New Jerusalem)*

The new life is described as being a new Jerusalem. We have seen the symbolism of this book reveal great truths all the way up to this point so there is no need to change now.

Those who are God's servants remain his servants even in this unveiling of the future promise. We see the angels who had the bowls now speaking again to the seer.

The thing which we see is the New Jerusalem. Jerusalem was always considered the holy city. It was the city of God, the place he chose. It was the location of the temple in the Old Testament days. It was the location of Jesus Christ's crucifixion and resurrection. It was the central city of the promised land. People understood Jerusalem as having special significance in God's eyes. Thus the eternal promise comes in the form of the New Jerusalem. This gives the people something with which they can compare it.

The picture revolves around the number twelve and its multiples and fractions. The church is the people of God and twelve is their number. If the people of God are gathered for a new life, it ought to be emphasized through this number. Twelve was the number of God's elect, the tribes, and the disciples. It is obvious then that the eternal dwelling place of his company of believers should center on that number.

The first aspect of this new place which strikes the seer is its radiance (Revelation 21:11). John picks up all the precious jewels and weaves them into a tremendous picture of radiance. This cannot be a literal scene, or the believers would end up with exactly the things Rome was trying to be. What this points out is the magnificent radiance one can expect in the presence of God. The human mind is limited to the beautiful things which we know on earth. We cannot begin to comprehend the greatness of God. Such things as pure gold surpass our imagination.

21:22-27 *(Worship in the New Jerusalem)*

Our first reaction, a very human reaction to verse 22, is "What, no temple?" Of course not! God is the temple. He does not need a building made with hands to symbolize his presence. He is in the midst of his people. Our whole lives become worship.

The thought of no sun or moon is inconceivable to us. But remember this is symbolic. God is everywhere. He is the center of this eternal life. His radiance shines (Revelation 21:23). We cannot understand this. We cannot logically and scientifically prove this. We accept it by faith. Our God is a god of power and creation. If he could bring life into existence once, he can do it again. It was he who created the sun and moon of the first life, and he will provide the sustenance of life in eternity.

Points To Ponder

Try to remember some of the promises in the opening verses of this chapter.

Why would heaven be described in such beautiful earthly terms?

What do you think heaven will be like?

What is the significance of there being no temple in the new city?

Chapter 22

22:1-5 *(Details of the City, People, and Living)*

There is a fantastic picture in Revelation 22:2 as the water, a precious commodity to the majority of the world and especially the Asia Minor area, flows right down the middle of the street. The tree of life (Genesis 2:9) is also present. It is not across the river unable to be reached but on both sides, accessible to all with its sustenance.

The dreaded nights with their insecure feelings are gone (Revelation 21:25 and 22:5). The majority of crime experienced on earth is committed at night. The sounds which we hear at night have added tension, because we can't see the source. The storms of night terrify us more than those of the day, because we can't see how much the wind is blowing, but we can see all the lightning. Think of the assurance one would feel without this fear. For some the night can be beautiful, but it seems that only happens when we behold the moon and the stars and sense God's greatness and presence. At times like that, we do not sense the night but we feel the strength of God.

How beautiful it will be when God is our light and we reign forever. Think a minute about that. God's presence with us, nothing unclean, water of life, tree of life, night fears gone, forever. Forever! Wow!

The limited human mind cries out: "How, where, when?" We quietly and skeptically think, "Prove it." But the God of creation needs no proof. The God of salvation has done his thing. And the Spirit battles within us not to ask earthly questions but simply trust. That trust is what Christ meant when he said that to children belongs the Kingdom of God.

22:6-7 *(I Am Coming Soon)*

As John develops his concluding remarks, he keeps us mindful of Christ's second coming (Revelation 22:7, 12, 20). Jesus himself spoke to his followers on earth with the words, "Watch therefore, for you do not know on what day your Lord is coming" (Matthew 24:42). John emphasizes that Jesus said he was coming soon.

Whether the second coming was to take place in John's lifetime, or whether it will take place in ours, should make no difference. The people of God should live expectantly. We are called to a response which should be no different if Christ returns tomorrow, next year, or the next century. Our response should be to live a life of obedience to God and love toward others.

Keeping the words of the prophecy of this book would include all the explicit instructions, such as those given to the seven churches in chapters 2 and 3, as well as the implicit instructions we feel in seeking to live opposite of the evil ways of the world condemned throughout this book by God's judgment.

22:8-9 *(Worship God)*

As we viewed the evil of the world coming under God's judgment in this book, we were continually made aware of the many idols which people worship. There is the greedy power that leads nations to war against nations. There are the riches and luxuries which people attempt to lay up for themselves. There are the many compromises which even the believers make in their faith to appease their friends. There are the shady deals of politics and many more.

To all of this John quotes the angel's words, "Worship God." Whenever we keep our focus on the one who has given us his all, even his Son, we can remain steadfast and true to the time of Christ's return.

22:10-13 *(Choosing Your Eternity)*

One must never lose sight of our own responsibility. It is not God who makes us bad, but it is we who choose this course. There is the continual battle or struggle within us between doing what we selfishly want and doing what we know is right.

Verse 12 reminds us that our reward is closely connected with our lifestyle or life purpose. Some would call it our doings or our actions. If we choose to forget God and serve ourselves, our recompense will be an eternity separated from that God. If we choose in this life to serve God, our eternity will be one of worship of that God.

22:14-15 ***(The Blessing and the Separation)***

Drawing together some previously used images and pictures, John quotes a blessing from God which connects our being washed in the blood of the Lamb with the promise of the tree of life and the new city.

Separated from this life with God are those who separated themselves in the earthly life by practicing falsehood.

22:16-17 ***(A Final Invitation)***

It is Jesus, God himself incarnate, crucified, and risen, who brought these words to the church. The church has as its objective to go and invite others. This book is not evangelistic in the normal understanding of the word. Very little of the content encourages people to turn around, repent, look to God. The majority of this book is devoted to telling it like it is and depicting the outcome of such living. Nevertheless, there is a certain evangelism implied. As long as we live on this earth, we can hear these judgments rumbling like thunder on the horizon and take advantage of all opportunities to invite others into the shelter of God. It's free, given by the grace of God. But we must be thirsty before we can drink.

22:18-19 ***(A Warning)***

These words have caused some people to shy away from this book for fear God will condemn them for misinterpretation. Our God is a God of love who never turns his back on those who seek him. To read his word is certainly to seek him, and we would not be condemned for doing that.

This warning could easily have applied to the carriers of this message. It could also have applied to the churches to whom it was sent. They might not have liked what it said about them and altered it before circulating it to their fellow believers in other communities. It could also apply to us, if we ever belittle the judgments as fairy tales. We must read the words as they are. Hear the promise and power of God. Understand the situation in which they were written, and interpret their meaning for our lives today.

If people alter this message to suit their own purpose, the consequence is the removal of their share of the tree of life. This is the strongest warning possible.

22:20-21 ***(The Constant Love of God)***

When we sense the promise of God for our eternity and know his love, "...in that while we were yet sinners Christ died for us" (Romans 5:8), we will expectantly look forward to Christ's return.

Jesus says he is coming soon. We answer, "Please do." And with a final benediction, the vision is closed. It is not to be hidden, but rather to be shared. It is our **hope** in time of trouble. It is our **promise** in time of conflict. It is our joyful **expectation** of a perfect new life in the presence of the God whom we love and serve as he has first loved us. It is reason for all of us to face the future with faith, hope, and trust.

Points To Ponder

How do you think John felt when this final portion of the vision was revealed to him? How do you feel reading it today?

Who is the center of focus in the final chapter? Why?

What is on both sides of the river? Do you see any significance to this?

When John fell down to worship what was he admonished to do?

What is Jesus' promise in this chapter and in the book?

Is he coming soon?

Epilogue

Is He Coming Soon?

The God of love, who created this world, died for its sins, and aids our struggle through his Spirit, will bring all things to completion. People were not created to die. Humankind was created and through birth we live in the chain of creation called procreation. All of us are born to live in harmony with our creator. Our ancestors chose in their own responsibility and of their own free choice to serve themselves. Had we lived then, we would have done the same thing, for our earthly life today gives evidence of that fact. The completion which God brings is not the end of life, but a new beginning. It will come when Christ returns and judgment is made.

The faithful of God who are washed in the blood of the Lamb can respond to this vision of John in just one way. **Amen. Come, Lord Jesus!**

CPSIA information can be obtained at www.ICGtesting.com
Printed in the USA
LVOW071148060412

276437LV00001B/19/P